CONTENTS

© Ward Lock Limited, 1993
A Cassell Imprint
Villiers House, 41-47 Strand, London WC2N 5JE

Based on *Creating A Home*
First Edition © Eaglemoss Publications Limited, 1986

ISBN 0 7063 7207 7

Printed in Spain by Cayfosa Industria Grafica

INTRODUCTION

The cost of restoring anything old and treasured can come high if you have to rely on the skills of a specialist – doing it yourself not only saves money but can also reward you with the satisfaction of making something as good as new.

Renovation around the home is the ideal reference book for every resourceful home owner who wants to restore elements in a period house or simply breathe new life into tired old furniture.

Renovation involves more than applying a lick of paint or giving an item a quick polish. It is a craft that takes time, patience and a degree of skill. But with dozens of quick professional tips and clear, concise explanations throughout, this book will give you the confidence to restore a whole range of items. Step-by-step instructions backed up with clear illustrations guide you through all the stages of a project. Any special materials or equipment required are outlined at the start of each chapter.

The first section of the book concentrates on the structure of your home, helping you revive decorative plaster cornice work, maintain a traditional fireplace and repair irreplaceable stained glass. Further chapters prove that broken china, worn textiles and chipped stone ornaments don't have to be consigned to the dustbin, if you're prepared to put time and effort into giving them a new lease of life.

Furniture in the family home has to work hard for a living and everyday wear and tear will, in time, mar its good looks. Neglected pieces of furniture are also often to be found languishing in junk shops at knock-down prices, and it's worth acquiring the basic knowledge to turn a bargain into a thing of beauty. The chapters on furniture renovation tell you all you need to know to repair hinges and runners, re-cane chairs, strip and polish old pine and restore traditional hardwoods.

Renovation around the home is the ideal manual for everyone who wants to make a home to be proud of, and then keep it that way.

Mending cornices and plasterwork

Decorative cornices and plasterwork are often spoilt by layers of paint and missing sections. By removing the choking paint and replacing the damaged sections, cornices (and intricate picture and mirror frames) can be restored.

Cornices

Beautifully moulded cornices on walls and ceilings give character to a room, yet the finer details of the cornice can often be blurred by layers of distemper (thickened water-based paint) or paint which has been allowed to build up over the years. However, with patience and a few simple tools, these layers can be removed to reveal the original moulding in all its glory.

If parts of the cornice are missing or damaged, these can be recast using a mould made from an undamaged section. A couple of coats of paint over the whole cornice will complete the renovation, giving it a bright, fresh look.

Preparing a cornice

To prepare a cornice before painting is a long and messy job, as the old layers of paint and grime need to be removed before painting can begin.

You will need
◇ Floor covering
◇ Bucket
◇ Sugar soap or soapy water
◇ Paint brush
◇ Nail brush or old toothbrush
◇ Old screwdriver or narrow chisel

1 Cover floor. Brush diluted sugar soap or warm, soapy water on to the cornice, using a paint brush. Leave to soak in for about 10-15 minutes.

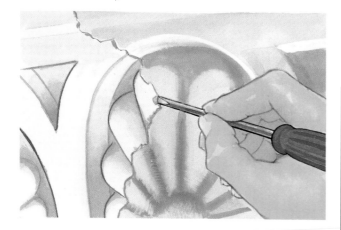

3 Gently sweep the exposed plaster with the nail brush — or use a toothbrush in the crevices — to remove any remaining flakes.

2 Take a pointed tool, such as an old screwdriver or narrow chisel, and carefully prise the paint away, turning the tool head gently in the paint. Take care not to dig at the paint in case the plaster becomes chipped or scratched.

Replacing sections of a plaster cornice

Plaster cornices were originally made in short lengths of about 12in (30cm) with S-shaped ends. Sections fitted together like a jigsaw, making the cornice simple to install. Likewise, it is easy to remove a section when a piece is needed to make a mould. The divisions between sections are usually revealed when the cornice is cleaned. The damaged section, plus an undamaged one, can then be taken down.

You will need
◇ Length of cornice in the design to be copied (see above)
◇ Silicone mould rubber RTV-700:

2-3lb (1.3kg) depending on cornice width
◇ Beta l curing agent (catalyst)
◇ Hard casting plaster: a 6lb (3kg) bag should be plenty for l length
◇ Box frame to fit cornice length
◇ Old narrow chisel or screwdriver
◇ Palette knife
◇ Mixing bowls
◇ Old spoon
◇ Weighing scales
◇ ½in (1.2cm) paint brush
◇ Piece of chalk
◇ Plaster coving adhesive
◇ Cellulose filler
◇ Fine glass paper

▽ *A three-sided mould is advisable on plaster pieces which are difficult to box snugly.*

Restoring a cornice

A damaged section of a cornice can be replaced by making a new length of cornice. This may sound like a daunting task, but the rubber moulding solutions now available from most DIY stores make it quite achievable. The moulding solution is poured around an undamaged section of cornice to form a mould for casting a new piece of plaster.

Materials and equipment

Moulding materials

Cold cure silicone rubber, also known as RTV-700, is the easiest material to use for making an accurate mould. A catalyst is added just before use. The catalyst dictates how long the rubber takes to dry and how thick it is. To make a solid block mould, use a catalyst which cures within 24 hours. With experience, a faster-drying, tougher rubber can be painted on to form a skin-like mould. This method is cheaper as it uses less rubber.

Box frame

In order to pour the mould, the cornice must be placed in a box frame. The cornice should fit snugly into the box frame, with the sides of the frame being 1in (2.5cm) higher than the depth of the cornice. It may be necessary to make a frame of the correct dimension to suit your section of cornice. Use heavy cardboard, reinforcing the joins with tape or wood.

Plaster

A white, fast-drying, hard casting plaster is needed for cornicing. It is important to add the powdered plaster to water slowly, stirring constantly until it is well mixed and of a thick creamy consistency that can be poured into the mould.

Fine surface cellulose filler can be used to cast a small section.

Adhesive

An adhesive recommended for fixing modern plaster coving is also a suitable choice for installing the traditional cornice. When the adhesive is quite dry, use cellulose filler to fill and cover any small cracks between the sections and between the wall and cornice.

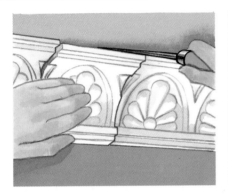

1 Gently prise away the length to be copied. Use an old chisel or screwdriver to loosen the sides, then insert a pliable tool like a palette knife between the cornice section and the wall, to loosen the back. Remove carefully.

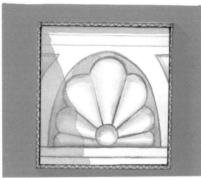

2 Place length of cornice, right side up, in the box frame. Empty rubber into mixing bowl and weigh it, then gently stir to ensure it is well mixed. Weigh catalyst: use 1 part of catalyst, to 10 parts of rubber solution. Add the catalyst to the rubber solution and mix well but carefully until colour is even. Fold in as little air as possible.

3 Brush a thin layer of rubber solution over the face of the cornice. This helps eliminate air bubbles on the surface. Slowly pour the solution into one corner of the container and allow it to flow around the design. When the pattern is half-covered, stop pouring and allow the mould to level off for a few moments. Start pouring again until the highest point of the design is covered by $\frac{1}{2}$in (1.2cm) of rubber. Leave the rubber solution to cure on a flat surface for 24 hours.

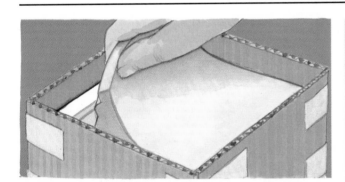

4 Pull mould gently away from the sides of the box, then peel it off the cornice length. Remove cornice section. If necessary wipe mould over with water to clean it. Dry and replace mould in box with the design uppermost.

5 Weigh the plaster. In a separate bowl place cold water in the ratio of 1 pint water to 3lb 9oz of plaster (1 litre water to 2.89kg of plaster). Add the plaster slowly to the water, stirring well, but gently, all the time.

6 Measure the thickness of the base of the original section of cornice. Make a chalk mark around the inside of the box this height above the highest point of the mould design. First brush some plaster over the mould face to eliminate air bubbles, then slowly pour the rest into the mould up to the chalk line. Leave for 30 minutes to set.

7 To remove plaster shape turn container upside down. With one hand support the cast, then tap the base and ease out the new section. Pull the mould off the cast and replace in container for reuse.

8 Put the cast length to one side and continue to make any further lengths of cornice needed. If necessary, gently file down the back to fit the space to which it will be attached. Lightly sand edges, ends and back surface of each length of cornice.

9 Using the screwdriver or old chisel, score scratch lines on the back of both the new section and the ceiling where it is to fit. These lines provide a key for the adhesive. Use plaster coving adhesive to fix the lengths in position, following the manufacturer's instructions.

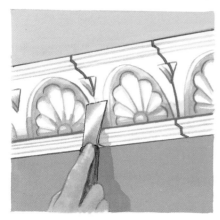

10 When the adhesive is dry, use cellulose filler to fill any cracks between lengths or at the sides of the cornice. Paint plaster as required.

Plaster frames

Old, ornate picture and mirror frames often become damaged in places. Like cornicing, a new piece can be cast in plaster using a mould taken from an identical section elsewhere on the frame.

Plasticine is an ideal moulding material for such small jobs. Work the Plasticine until it is pliable. Press a piece ½in (1.2cm) thick on to the area to be copied. Leave the Plasticine until cold and set, then remove carefully. The pattern should be perfectly reproduced in the Plasticine which can now be used as a mould. This type of mould does not need to be boxed.

The new plaster decoration can be cut to fit the space with a craft knife, or sanded, then glued in place. Seal the plaster with a clear sealer before applying the finish which is usually gold. Wax or paint the new section to match the rest of the frame, and again afterwards if it is gold, to retard tarnishing.

▽ *Chips out of mirror and picture frames make a fine decorative piece look shabby. Small pieces can be replaced by making a mould in Plasticine and casting from this.*

Renovating fireplaces

A glowing hearth is a focal point in any room,
yet the potential of this delightful feature is often ignored.
Many marks and surface damage can be treated to
improve the look of the piece, while regular cleaning will
maintain the lustre of the fireplace.

△ The different materials — ceramic tiles, wood and cast iron —
in this fireplace require individual attention.

An open fireplace gives a room an obvious point of interest, whether it is still used for its original purpose or has become a purely decorative feature. It is important to make the most of such an attraction by ensuring that it always looks its best.

Unfortunately, many original fireplaces become damaged, marked and shabby over the years because of wear and neglect, and others are covered by layers of paint. Many small jobs, such as removing marks, filling cracks and surface cleaning, can be carried out by amateurs, though some restoration work, such as burnishing cast iron, is best left to the experts.

Fireplace surrounds are made of stone, timber, metal, brick or tile, or a combination of these materials. Regular cleaning and an additional annual overhaul will help to keep the surrounds in good condition.

Preparation

Carry out any renovation work in spring or summer not in winter when the fireplace is most likely to be in use. Renovation work can be messy, and the room must be well ventilated to allow fumes and dust to escape. Have the chimney swept before starting work.

Make sure you know what type of surface you are dealing with, as the wrong cleaning method is likely to do more harm than good. If the surface has been painted, gently scrape away the paint in an inconspicuous area to find out what the fireplace itself is made of.

Do the messiest work first. For example, if the insert is cast iron and the facade marble, begin by cleaning and blacking the cast iron before cleaning the marble. Never work on a fireplace with a gas or real fire burning. Always make sure the surround is cold before starting your renovation work.

Removing paint

Layers of paint can obscure rich details and mouldings. Stripping off the paint and restoring the original surface can transform the appearance of a fireplace, but remember, this can be a gamble — you may find that the original surface was painted over to conceal marks or faults such as cracks. Some of these problems can be treated, while others add to the appeal of the fireplace. If the surface is very badly damaged, consider repainting it.

Cast iron

Cast iron has either a blacked or burnished finish. Many fireplaces have a blacked insert (the part immediately round the fire) with the facade in another material.

Paint can be stripped off cast iron and the exposed surface then coated with blacklead to give a matt black finish. Buff over the blacked surface with a soft brush from time to time to keep a smart appearance.

Burnishing gives the surface a wonderful metallic grey lustre but is extremely difficult to do and is best left to the experts.

Stripping cast iron
You will need
◇ Dust sheet
◇ Mild paint stripper
◇ Paint scraper and shavehook
◇ Bowl
◇ Wet-and-dry paper
◇ Blacklead
◇ White spirit
◇ Paint brush
◇ Shoe brush

1 Cover the surrounding area with a dust sheet and open windows. Brush on mild paint stripper. When the paint starts to bubble, scrape it all off, using the shavehook for detailed areas.

2 When all the paint has been removed, clean down the surface with white spirit. Rub off any rust marking the surface using wet-and-dry paper. Mix the blacklead with white spirit to make a liquid. Paint this mixture over the metal surface and leave to dry: allow about 2 hours.

3 Polish up the blacking with a shoe brush kept specially for this purpose.

Rust marks

Blacking does not make metal rustproof, so keep water well away from the fireplace. If rust does form, sand down the area using wet-and-dry paper until all the rust has gone. Black the area again. On a burnished finish, sand back, then rub in a little WD40 using a clean, soft cotton cloth.

TIP	MARKS

Keep liquids such as water, tea and coffee away from the fireplace as these are likely to stain the surface.

Timber surrounds
Cleaning
The timber used around fireplaces is kiln dried, so it will not be affected by the heat of the fire. Dust and polish with a wax furniture polish regularly to feed the wood and bring out the grain patterning. For further details on removing marks and mending dents and chips in wood, see pages 46 and 50-51.

For a more thorough clean, use a soft brush and warm water to remove dirt from nooks and crannies. Do not saturate the surface as this may cause the wood to warp or crack with the heat of a fire. To finish, polish when thoroughly dried.

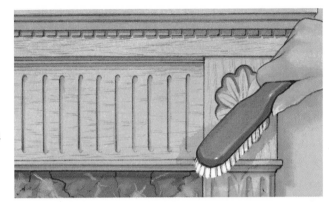

Stripping timber
To strip a wooden fireplace facade effectively, it is best to have it professionally dipped in a caustic bath. The fireplace will have to be removed from its setting for this. Sometimes, gesso or plaster has been used in details on the facade. This will come away from the frame if dipped, so make sure that the entire frame is made of wood before deciding on the course of action.

The layers of paint can be thinned by rubbing them down with glass paper. Alternatively, use an electric sander — this will make the job much quicker and easier. Be sure to keep the surface even when using the sander. Then repaint it using a heat-resistant paint. Thin the paint if necessary to prevent a thick build-up.

Marble
Paint can be stripped off marble using a proprietary paint stripper. Make sure the stripper used is compatible with marble. For further details on how to remove stains from marble see pages 29-31.

If the marble is particularly badly marked, employ a professional restorer to treat the surface with a commercial poltice.

Once stripped, the surface needs to be rubbed down and waxed. Do not press to hard on the corners and edges as the marble is likely to crumble away.

▽ Timber fireplace facades are often painted to complement the colour scheme of a room.

Stripping marble
You will need
◇ Dust cloth
◇ Paint stripper
◇ Paint brush
◇ Thin-bladed scraper
◇ Medium and fine wet-and-dry glass paper
◇ Marble wax
◇ Clean cotton cloths
◇ Electric drill with buffer attachment

1 Cover surrounding area with dust cloth and open windows. Apply paint stripper and leave for specified time. Gently scrape off stripper and paint with a thin-bladed scraper. Take care not to dig into the marble with the scraper, as it is easily chipped.

2 Wipe down the surface with a clean, damp cloth. Sand down using medium wet-and-dry paper. Wipe the surface. Change to fine wet-and-dry and using a little warm water, give the marble a final rubbing down.

3 Clean off all traces of dust. Apply marble wax with a soft, dry cloth, using plenty of pressure. Polish using a buffer head on a drill for extra sheen.

Brick
This is hard wearing and does not damage easily. Clean with a soft brush dipped in warm water or a proprietary cleaner. Never use soapy water as it will leave behind a scum on the surface.

For bad stains, use a solution of one part hydrochloric acid (spirits of salt) to 15 parts water. Put the water into a container first and then add the acid. Wearing rubber gloves, brush the solution well over the stained area and leave to soak in for 20 minutes. Wash over the area with clean, cold water.

Tiles

The small, more modern ceramic tiles used round the facade and hearth often come loose or crack. Remove a tile only if it is badly damaged, as this is a tricky operation and the surrounding tiles may become damaged at the same time. When replacing tiles, make sure the new ones are the same colour, size and thickness as the others.

The larger, more decorative tiles often seen in panels set into the sides of a surround are almost impossible to replace individually. A whole panel usually has to be replaced and the best option is to get a professional to do this. Original and replica tiles are widely available through tile and specialist fireplace shops.

Cleaning tiles

Wash over ceramic tiles with hot water and detergent. Wipe over with clean water. Gently rub over more stubborn stains with wire wool.

Replacing tiles
You will need
◇ Matching tile
◇ Hammer and chisel
◇ Adhesive
◇ Grouting
◇ Plastic adhesive/grout spreader

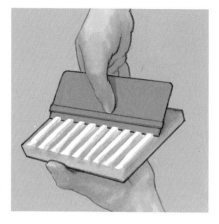

2 Scrape away any cement or adhesive left in the recess in order to even up the surface. Try the new tile for size in the hole. Take it out and spread adhesive evenly over the back of the tile and the surface to which it will be stuck. Do not get adhesive on the front of the tile.

3 Gently press in place with fingers. Clean off any visible adhesive with a cloth. Leave to dry for about 12 hours.

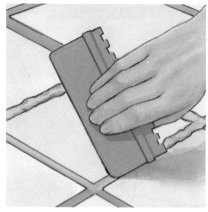

4 Spread heat resistant grout over the gaps. Wipe off excess grout with a cloth. Run the rounded corner of the scraper along the cracks to press in and smooth over the grouting. Wipe away unwanted traces of grout.

Loose tiles

Clean any remaining adhesive off the back of the tile and out of the recess, then replace the tile following steps 2-4 above.

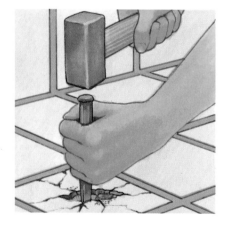

1 Starting in the centre, chip out the damaged tile using the hammer and chisel. Take great care chipping around the edge not to damage the adjacent tiles.

△ All that glistens must be well cared for.

Opening up a fireplace

Many homes have boarded up chimney places which can be opened up and restored to their former glory. If the grate is to glow with either a real or gas fire, call in a professional to check on the chimney to ensure it is safe to use.

Behind the board, the original fireplace may be in one piece and only need cleaning up. It is more common to find that the hood and bars or grate have been taken off or are missing. These will have to be re-attached by a professional or new ones bought. Weigh up the costs of restoration carefully — it may be cheaper to buy a replacement fireplace.

Replacing window panes

*A broken pane of glass spoils the view from a
window and is a real hazard in a glazed door. Instead of getting
the glass replaced by a professional glazier — who is
likely to present you with a surprisingly large bill — it is
perfectly possible to do the job yourself.*

Replacing a pane of glass in a
window or a glazed door is well
within the reach of most people,
though it does require patience,
care and accuracy.

As glass can cause serious injury,
it is important to take a few simple
safety precautions before starting
work. When you are handling
broken glass, always wear thick
gloves, such as gardening gloves,
and stout shoes to avoid injury.
Wear a pair of goggles or sun-
glasses to protect your eyes. Lay
newspaper on the floor by the
window to catch any glass. Wrap

△ *A cracked or broken pane of
glass will mar the look of doors,
cupboards or windows. It takes little
effort to take out the damaged piece
and put in a new one.*

broken glass in several sheets of
newspaper before disposing of it.

Replacing broken glass
Wooden window or door frame
The glass fits into a rebate (groove). Use a metal tape measure to measure the opening. To allow for expansion, the height and width of the new glass sheet should be $^3/_{16}$in (5mm) less than the opening.

You will need
◇ Pane of glass
◇ Putty
◇ Glazier's nails
◇ Primer and small brush
◇ Glass cutter
◇ Hammer
◇ Pincers

◇ Sandpaper
◇ Chisel
◇ Putty knife
◇ Square-ended filling knife
◇ Soft brush
◇ Paint
◇ Strong gloves

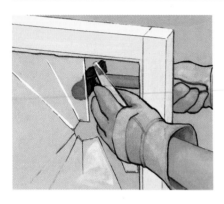

1 Wearing strong gloves to protect your hands, carefully remove the damaged glass using a glass cutter and hammer. To reduce the risk of injury, work from the top of the pane downwards. For details see page 19.

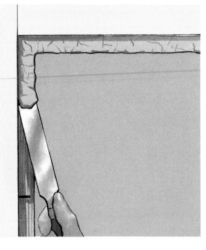

2 Close the window or door and scrape out all the old putty. Use a chisel to do this.

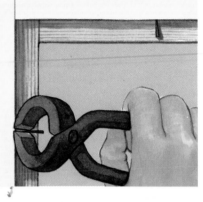

3 Use pincers to pull out the glazier's nails. Clean the rebate thoroughly with sandpaper. Then brush out any debris and paint with primer. Leave to dry thoroughly for several hours.

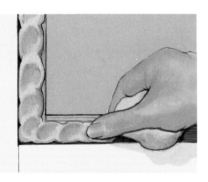

4 Roll and knead the putty in your hands to make it soft and flexible. Then press the putty into the window frame rebate using your thumb and forefinger.

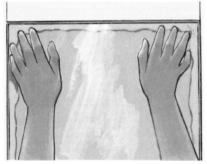

5 Lift the glass up to the window and press firmly into place. Press the edges into the putty — do not apply pressure to the centre of the glass.

6 Using the edge of a chisel, tap glazier's nails into rebate.

7 Spread more putty around the edges of the glass, using a putty knife to smooth the surface level with the rebate. Mitre the putty neatly at each corner.

8 Use the edge of the putty knife to remove excess putty from the glass. Clean off any fingerprints.

9 Leave putty to harden for a week or two. To finish, paint the putty, taking a very narrow line of paint on to the glass.

Metal window frame or door
With a metal-framed window or door, the glass must be secured with a special type of self-hardening putty for metal frames, plus wire clips instead of glazier's nails. Follow the instructions for the wood-framed window, omitting the sanding. After removing putty and cleaning the recess, paint with aluminium paint.

TIP   BIG PANES

◇ Although it is possible to replace most standard-sized panes of glass yourself, leave very large picture windows and sliding doors to a professional glazier.

◇ If the window is high up and in a difficult location, call in a professional rather than run the risk of injury.

Repairing stained glass

*A broken pane in a stained glass window automatically
draws the eye, no matter how beautiful the overall design. Putting
in a new piece takes time and care but gives
a very satisfying result. Other minor repairs can have an equally
reviving effect on the window.*

Many houses have stained glass panels in their windows and doors. They are usually positioned so that the light brings out the full richness of the colours, but this also shows up dirt and damage.

Windows and doors are vulnerable to wear and tear from the weather outside and from knocks and vibrations inside. Panes of glass can become cracked and the came (lead strips used to hold the glass in place)

can be split or weakened.

Small faults are often left because they seem difficult to mend, yet with patience and concentration they can be repaired — and a good clean can have an astonishing effect.

Cleaning

Clean gently, and avoid putting pressure on the glass particularly if the window is old. First dust the surface with a soft-bristled paint brush. This will get the dust and most of the dirt out of the numerous corners and crevices round the leading.

For extra sparkle and to remove stubborn marks, use a solution of liquid detergent and a few drops of ammonia in hot water. Wipe over the glass with a chamois leather, then remove any traces of the solution with hot water. Finally, wipe with a damp chamois.

Repairing

Small repairs — such as covering cracks or replacing a couple of pieces of glass — can be carried out with the window in place. For large scale repairs it will be necessary to take the window out of its setting so that the job can be done on a work surface.

If a window is very old or valuable, it is better to seek professional advice unless you have a great deal of experience of working with stained glass. Always be careful when working with glass, as edges and slivers can give nasty cuts.

Covering cracks

With a small crack, it may not be worth the effort of replacing the glass. However, even a small crack is a weak point and, if left untreated, it is likely to crack further. Adhesive can be used to bind and strengthen small cracks. Use either an epoxy resin or, better still, a clear anaerobic glue (which will not discolour but needs careful handling as it can set in just a few seconds).

Small, clean breaks can be filled in the same way. Once treated with adhesive, the crack can be hidden under a strip of self-adhesive lead.

You will need
◇ Adhesive
◇ Artists' brush
◇ Single-edged razor
◇ Masking tape
◇ Self adhesive lead strip (optional)

Replacing broken glass

Glass pieces with holes or multiple cracks will need to be replaced with new glass. The lead will inevitably be slightly scarred by this disturbance, so work from the outside when repairing a stained glass window. With doors, work from whichever side is least on view.

When buying the replacement glass, remove the piece of glass that needs replacing and take it with you. It is more important to match the colour than the texture of the glass as the eye is drawn to colour first. If this is mismatched the repair will immediately be obvious.

If the pattern in the window is symmetrical, and you cannot quite match the glass, it may be worth replacing the piece opposite the damaged one as well to retain the balance of the pattern.

Making a template of the shape to be cut in cheap, plain glass reduces the chance of making a mistake when cutting the more expensive coloured glass. The more experienced cutter may prefer to cut the coloured glass straight from a card template.

Tools

Tools required include: lead knife; glass cutter, preferably with a cutting wheel, and a lathekin. Pliers are needed for cutting and loosening glass. Ordinary flat-nosed pliers may be used, but specialist pliers make life much easier. Grozening pliers for nibbling glass edges and glass breaking pliers are recommended.

Method

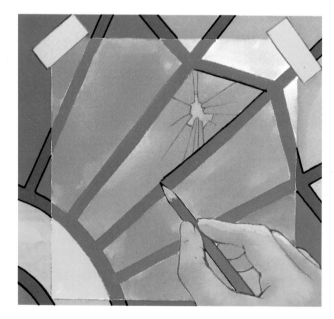

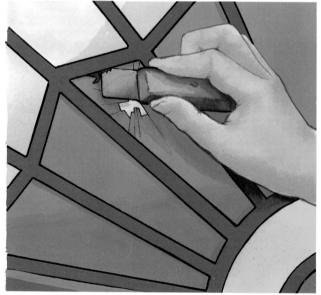

1 Attach a piece of tracing paper over the damaged area. Using a soft pencil or crayon, make a rubbing or mark the outline of the area. Put this copy on top of a piece of card and trace around the line of the glass shape to be replaced. Add $^{1}/_{16}$ in (2mm) all round. Cut out the shape on the card as a template.

2 From the external side of the window, start to work the leading knife under the lead came to loosen the cement. Slowly work along all the sides that hold in the piece of damaged glass.

To seal a crack use an artists' brush to paint adhesive over the damaged line. Make sure the crack is well filled, then leave to dry. When set, carefully scrape away excess glue globules from the glass surface with a single-edged razor blade.

To seal a clean break join the break with adhesive, applied with an artists' brush. Put masking tape across join to hold it in place while adhesive dries, then remove it. Remove excess glue when dried as described under sealing a crack. To cover the repair line, cut two pieces of self adhesive lead to required length. Stick on each side of glass across the join.

Using a glass cutter

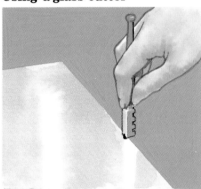

Keep your glass cutter well lubricated when not in use. Store in a jar, wheel down, on an absorbent pad soaked in a solution of one part light household oil, two parts white spirit. Never try to use a blunt cutter and once you have made a score never go over it again.

To hold a cutter put the handle in the 'V' between the first and second fingers of your writing hand. Grasp the lower part of the handle between thumb and forefinger.

You will need
◇ Tracing paper
◇ Soft pencil or crayon
◇ Glass cutter
◇ Glass cutters
◇ Leading knife
◇ Pliers
◇ Lathekin
◇ Clear glass
◇ Matching coloured glass
◇ Hammer and screwdriver (optional)
◇ Putty
◇ Putty knife
◇ Black paint powder

3 When as much cement as possible has been removed, lever up the lead until the sides are at an angle of 90° or more to the glass.

4 To remove damaged glass, score the surface with the glass cutter and then tap it with the rounded end of the cutter. Work the pieces out using pliers. Fingers may be needed for some, but be very careful.

5 To clear out glass still trapped between the lead, particularly in the corners, put the head of a screwdriver into the crevice and gently tap the end with a hammer to shatter the glass. Care must be taken here as too much force may damage the glass on the surrounding sides. Scrape the glass free with the screwdriver's head. Using as little pressure as possible, clear out any cement left on the lower lead ledge.

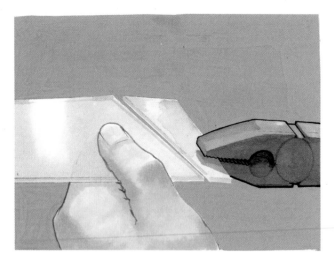

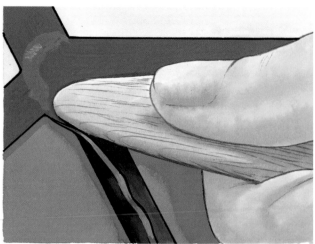

6 Try out the card template in the hole and adjust as necessary. Put the template under a small sheet of plain glass and score round the shape with glass cutter. Holding the glass firmly next to the score in one hand, use a pair of plate pliers to carefully break the glass along the line. Any uneven edges can be gradually nibbled away using grozening pliers. Make sure the glass template fits the hole.

7 Hold the glass template on the coloured glass and score around it. Cut out the coloured shape. Place it on the lower lead ledge. Fold the top came flat over the glass by drawing the lathekin repeatedly along the length of the cames. Gently tap any stubborn raised areas with a small-headed hammer. Make sure the back of the window is well supported while you do this.

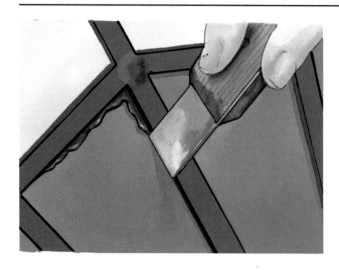

8 Mix up some putty and darken it with a little black paint powder. Push this under the cames on both sides of the glass using a putty knife. Carefully remove any excess from the glass.

Replacing old cement

Sometimes the cement between the came and the glass crumbles away, leaving the glass loose. New putty can be put in by first cleaning out the old residue and then replacing it, as described in steps 2 and 8.

Repairing damaged cames

If a came has broken in two it can be soldered back together. The best type of solder to use is a mixture of 60 per cent tin, 40 per cent lead. Before the solder is used, a flux has to be applied to the lead to make the solder easier to work. Use either a tallow flux or oleic acid available from good hardware stores. Always do soldering work in a well ventilated room.

You will need ◇ Soldering iron
◇ Flux ◇ Solder

1 First clean the surface of the lead thoroughly with a wire brush and make sure the lead is lying flat. If it is not, press it down with a lead knife. Apply the flux.

| **TIP** | **SOLDERING** |

For those unfamiliar with soldering, cover the glass around the area to be worked with masking tape to prevent any of the solder getting on the glass.

Never leave a hot soldering iron unattended or lying down, as this can cause a fire or result in someone burning themselves.

Never let the iron get overheated. Either use it — this will take away the heat — or make sure it is switched off.

2 Put a drop of melted solder on the join, shape and smooth it with the soldering iron.

Mending china

*Broken china need not always be consigned to the dustbin —
mending a straightforward break is a simple task
that takes only time and patience.*

What is china?

The term china is used today to encompass a wide range of materials, from heavy glazed earthenwares to delicate porcelain. The very properties which make china attractive and durable also make it brittle and prone to breakage, and a small tumble can easily cause a precious possession to shatter.

A broken china object is invariably irreplaceable — whether old or new it is virtually impossible to find a perfect match for a favourite tea service or replace single and highly treasured items such as ornaments or vases.

However, with a little time and patience it is possible to mend even the most fragmented piece and restore it to pristine condition.

Gathering the pieces

It is essential, when any breakage occurs, to gather up every fragment of china, no matter how small. Otherwise there is a risk that your piece will be incomplete. Once you have picked up all the pieces lay the sections on a clean surface, placing them together like a jigsaw puzzle to check that everything is there. If you don't plan to make the repair immediately, put all the pieces in a box or bag to ensure that nothing gets lost.

Supporting your repair

When you glue your sections together you can feel with your fingers when the join is perfect, but unless properly supported there is always the risk that they will slide apart slightly while drying. The best way to prevent this is to support the pieces so that the force of gravity keeps them in the correct position without the need to hold them in place. The most versatile form of support is the sand bed (see opposite).

Materials and equipment
Glues

Before the invention of modern glues, broken china had to be repaired with a sticky handmade mixture, and if it was to be used, riveted together with ugly iron or copper pins. The piece retained its serviceability, but frequently ruined the look of the dinner or tea service to which it belonged. Today, there is a wide range of adhesives on the market which are suitable for mending all types of china.

Epoxy resin adhesives These come in two separate tubes whose contents have to be mixed together. A chemical reaction between the two causes the mixture to harden. Standard epoxy resin sets in about 5-6 hours, but quicker setting resins are available which are better suited to small, delicate fractures. It is a good idea to add a small amount of coloured pigment to your mixture (available from good art shops and specialist suppliers) to match your china as epoxy resin yellows with age.

Cyanoacrylate adhesives These are more commonly known as super glues. Their quick drying time makes them ideal for mending small, shattered sections as they can be hand held until set, but it is essential to have a steady hand as mistakes are easy to make. These are not suitable for thicker, earthenware-type china.

Polyvinyl acetate adhesive This is a water-based glue which is ideal for earthenware.

With care, these adhesives will mend a simple break almost invisibly. Decorative wall plates can look as good as new, but although the bonding is strong, care must be taken when mending part of a dinner service; try to avoid using the china every day as even the most expertly repaired breaks can eventually absorb dirt. Wash all mended pieces by hand.

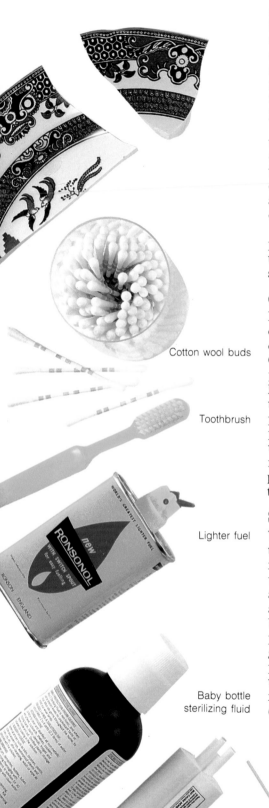

Cotton wool buds

Toothbrush

Lighter fuel

Baby bottle
sterilizing fluid

Alternative
quick-drying
adhesive

Powdered
pigment

Blades

Masking tape

Two-part epoxy
resin adhesive

Matchsticks

Sand bed

This is simply a box (such as a shoe box) or bowl filled with a finger's depth of sand into which drying pieces can be placed at an angle until the glue has set. Gravity helps to hold the pieces in position so there is less risk of the mend sliding apart while setting.

This method can be used for almost any kind of break and is particularly useful for odd shapes such as cup handles. However, take great care to keep grains of sand away from the repair – if they get embedded in the glue, they will spoil an otherwise perfect repair.

Sand bed

Mending a china plate

Preparation and patience are the secrets of a successful china repair. Work on a clean surface and make sure that once glued, you can leave your freshly mended sections in a position where they will be undisturbed for about eight hours until dry.

You will need
◇ Cotton wool buds
◇ Cellulose paint thinner or lighter fuel
◇ Soft cloth
◇ Baby bottle sterilizing fluid, denture cleaner or washing powder
◇ Powdered pigments
◇ Matchsticks
◇ Blade or scalpel
◇ Masking tape
◇ An old saucer
◇ Two-part epoxy resin adhesive
◇ Sand bed

Cleaning china

If your piece is old, or has been in a position where it has accumulated years of dust and dirt, the pieces may need cleaning before you start to assemble them.

1 Surface dirt and stains can be removed by immersing your piece in a bowl of baby bottle sterilizing fluid or denture cleaner. After a few minutes remove the china from the solution and wipe dry with a soft cloth.

2 Any dirt and grease that may have accumulated on the broken edges will prevent the glue from adhering properly. Clean any dirty edges thoroughly with a cotton wool bud dipped in lighter fuel or cellulose paint thinner, then put aside to dry.

Gluing china

Assemble all your freshly cleaned pieces on a clean work surface near to your sand bed (which must be in a position where it won't be disturbed for at least eight hours). Lay them out like a jigsaw puzzle to make it perfectly clear which order they fit together. Start by gluing the pieces nearest the rim and work inwards until you have only two large pieces. A multiple break may take some time to reassemble — don't be tempted to take shortcuts as this could lead to a shoddy repair.

1 Mix up a small quantity of two-part epoxy resin on an old saucer, following the manufacturer's instructions. Depending on the predominant colour of the glaze on your plate, add a tiny sprinkle of coloured pigment (just enough to tint the glue, so that it appears whitish but not enough to weaken the adhesion) and stir in to the resin.

2 Using a matchstick, wipe a small amount of tinted glue along the edges of the first two pieces of broken china.

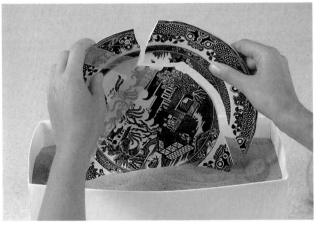

3 Carefully place the pieces together and hold for a few minutes until they have adhered. It may be necessary to place them in the sand tray until they are completely dry, but make sure you cover each side of the join with masking tape to prevent the sand from sticking to the glue. Once your first two pieces have dried, continue to build up your broken section until it is complete.

4 Bed the solid section of the plate firmly in the sand tray. Place at such an angle that the mended section sits happily on top (even if only for a few seconds) without falling off. Then apply glue to each side and stick carefully together. Cover the join with strips of masking tape to hold the two sides firmly together while the glue sets. Leave undisturbed for a minimum of eight hours.

5 When the glue has thoroughly dried, remove the plate from the sand bed and peel off the masking tape. Remove any excess glue with a blade or scalpel. Avoid scraping any paint or glaze.

TIP ALTERNATIVE SUPPORT

No two pieces of china break in the same manner, and therefore a method which will support one kind of break will not work for another. A straightforward single crack is best held together on a wooden board using a circle of nails and several elastic bands. Position the nails in a circle slightly larger than the piece, then stretch elastic bands across to hold it firmly.

Chips in china

*Chips in a favourite piece of china are
common, and professional restoration can be costly.
As long as the piece is of no particular value,
there is no reason why you cannot successfully repair
small chips yourself at home.*

Rebuilding missing areas in china may seem a daunting task. However, a little patience and a steady hand are all the skills you need to enable you to carry out the techniques shown here.

Small chips on rims can often be rebuilt using a 'support' taped to the underside of the rim to hold the filler in place. (Replacing larger or intricately shaped pieces is much more difficult and requires a mould.) Before you mend a piece of china remember that many antique pieces can be devalued by home repairs. China that is of any value should always be taken to a professional restorer.

Materials and equipment
Fillers
These are used to replace the missing area of china. In general you should always choose a filler that is slightly softer than the material you are working on. This will allow you to rub down any excess filler without damamging the surrounding area.

Plaster of Paris and cellulose fillers These are relatively soft materials and are generally used to fill glazed earthenware or porcelain that is for decorative use only. Fine grade cellulose wall filler (such as Polyfilla) is plaster with a cellulose filler which provides better adhesion. As Plaster of Paris and cellulose fillers are mixed with water, the broken edges of the object should be brushed with water before application. This prevents any additional water being drawn into the body of the earthenware. These fillers can be smoothed down with fine abrasive papers to provide an ideal surface for painting on, or they can be tinted with dry pigments prior to application.

Epoxy glue or putty (and polyester resin, such as car body fillers). These are harder materials and can be used on hard baked non-porous ceramics such as porcelain. They are available, ready-made, from hardware stores, and come in two tubes which are then mixed together in equal quantities. You can also make your own putty by mixing epoxy resin glue with whiting (powdered chalk), talc or kaolin (because koalin is grey, you may need to add titanium dioxide pigment to provide an white base). Make up the glue according to manufacturer's instructions (add titanium dioxide if required) then mix in the powder — small quantities at a time — to form a putty-like consistency. The putty can be tinted with pigments before application. Epoxy putty has a high adhesive quality, remains pliable for about an hour, during which time some basic shaping can be undertaken, and hardens within 12 hours. Despite its tough exterior the putty, once hard, can be sanded down.

Supports
Many chips can be mended using a support fixed to the back of the missing area — the filler is then pressed into the resulting space. Small chips can be backed with layers of masking tape, larger areas with Plasticine which is taped or held in place.

Abrasive papers
Use medium to fine glasspaper to remove excess filler and finish with fine grade glasspaper (sometimes known as flour paper) or plastic-backed silicone carbide paper. Use a small square of paper cut from the larger sheet, then fold it in half so that a single edge can be used to rub down the surface. This safeguards against scratching the surrounding glaze.

Pigments
For a professional finish you will either need to tint the filler to tone with the surrounding area or paint the finished restoration.

Dry artist's powder pigments come in a wide range of colours

Mending a wall plate

When carrying out any repairs, always work in a well-ventilated room as some of the chemicals used are potentially dangerous (check the packaging for information). Make sure you have plenty of room in which to work and that there is a good light source (preferably a natural light source).

You will need
- ◇ Artist's powder pigments
- ◇ Artist's brushes
- ◇ Medium and fine glasspaper
- ◇ Filler
- ◇ Cold curing glaze
- ◇ Thinner
- ◇ Plasticine
- ◇ Masking tape
- ◇ Cling film
- ◇ Palette knife
- ◇ Piece of thick white card or old ceramic tile
- ◇ Tracing materials (optional)
- ◇ Cleaning fluids

Repairing the chip

1 Make a mould by pressing Plasticine over an unbroken area of plate (this should be a similar shape to the broken area), sandwiching a piece of cling film between the Plasticine and the plate.

2 Peel the Plasticine away from the back of the plate using the cling film to ease it away from the surface. Align the Plasticine with the damaged edge of the plate.

and are available from artist's suppliers. They can be used for both tinting and painting. When painting, mix the powder with glaze and thin with a little solvent if necessary.

Acrylic paints are mixed with water and can be bought at most art shops. They are ideal for painting surface designs. Once the paint is dry it can be sealed with a coat of clear glaze if necessary.

Metallic powder paints can be used to simulate gilding and are applied in the same way as artist's powder paints or as pens. They are available from artist's suppliers and model shops.

Other paints include enamel paints, artist's oil colours, tubes of water colour and car body paint.

Glaze

Some restorers prefer to use glaze that requires firing (reheating — which is potentially damaging to the object). However, you will find it easier if you use a cold setting glaze such as a polyurethane coating. This cures (sets) by the addition of a small amount of hard-ener. It is available in clear or white. Clear glaze can be applied as a final coating over hand-painted designs. You can buy glaze from most hardware stores — they also stock an accompanying thinner for cleaning brushes.

Apply the glaze using a small brush and 'feather' it on to the undamaged glaze so that there is no visible join. If you need a slightly coloured glaze, tint it with powder pigments.

Brushes

Use good quality artist's brushes — preferably sable brushes — and choose a smaller size than you might feel necessary.

Painting and tinting

Whether working on a plain or patterned piece you will need to match the filler to its surround. Plain or background colours can sometimes be reproduced by tinting the filler before application, while any design will need to be painted in by hand once the repair has been completed (see overleaf).

Choosing colours

No matter what medium you choose, you are unlikely to get a ready-made colour match and will need to experiment by mixing various colours together. As a general guide, buy colours most prominently found in china — black, white, red, blue and a selection of yellows and browns. From this base you should be able to mix the colour you require. Mix colours on a piece of paper or an old tile and test on a piece of white paper.

Tinting

Plaster of Paris and cellulose filler Add dry pigment to the powdered filler before mixing with water. When dry, the filler will look considerably lighter than when wet, so remember to make allowances when adding pigment. Adding too much pigment will prevent the filler from setting.

Epoxy putty Mix the glue components together and tint with powdered pigment before adding filler. Kaolin darkens the finished colour.

Preparation

Chipped china soon becomes discoloured — especially those pieces that are still in use. Before you can carry out any restoration you must ensure that the broken surface is completely free of dirt and grime otherwise you will be left with an ugly line around the join.

Many pieces come clean when immersed in baby bottle sterilizing fluid or denture cleaner (for detailed advice on cleaning, see page 23).

However, more stubborn stains may require bleaching. Use a mixture of hydrogen peroxide (available from most chemists) or household bleach and ammonia.

This mixture should only be used to bleach earthenware as it is much too strong to be used on delicate porcelain pieces.

1 Soak the piece in water (to prevent the stain being drawn into the earthenware) and remove. Mix one part bleach with three parts water. Add a few drops of ammonia.

2 Use tweezers to dip pieces of cotton wool in the solution. Apply them to the stained area. Leave in place for a few hours. Repeat if necessary, soaking the piece before each application.

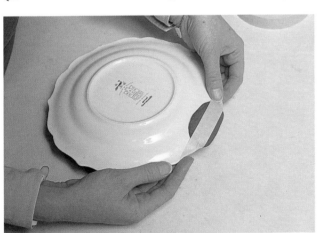

3 Secure the Plasticine in place with strips of masking tape. Make sure that it extends beyond the rim of the plate.

4 Make up a little filler and tint it if required (or paint the background colour later). With a palette knife, press the filler into the chip, building it up in layers to just above the rim.

Finishing the plate

When painting, you will not only have to duplicate the design but also the 'depth' of the pattern. If a pattern is slightly raised, extra layers of paint will need to be added to create the desired effect. Always 'feather' the new colour slightly over the existing design so that the old and new colours blend leaving no visible join.

Mix the colours required with a small amount of glaze — if they seem rather thick, dilute with a drop or two of thinner. Test each colour on an old tile or piece of white card and then, if possible, on the plate itself. Apply the colour to a glazed area so that you can wipe it off afterwards.

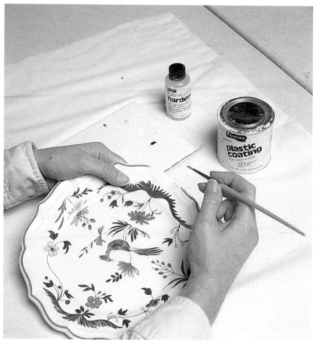

1 Once the filler has hardened, use medium to fine glasspaper to remove excess filler. Take care not to scratch the glaze and curve the rim to match the rest of the rim. Repeat with fine glasspaper so that the filler is flush with the rest of the surface.

2 Using a small brush, paint in any background colour, making sure that the filler is evenly covered and that the edges are blended with the original background colour. Leave to dry.

3 Using a fine brush, carefully paint in the design, blending the edges (allow one colour to dry before adding any others). Once the design is complete, lightly smooth down with very fine glasspaper. Apply a thin layer of clear glaze and leave to dry.

Tracing designs

Simple patterns and designs can usually be painted freehand. However, you may find it easier to trace more complicated designs from an undamaged area.

1 Find an undamaged area that has the same (or similar) design as your missing piece. Cover it with tracing paper, fix in position with masking tape and trace off the design.

2 Remove the tracing and scribble on the reverse side before placing it right side up on the restored area. Secure with tape and retrace over the outline.

Painting hints

◇ Practise creating shapes on a suitable surface before applying paint to the plate: have a selection of fine brushes and where possible, create outlines and shapes with a single brush stroke.

◇ When painting in designs, the paint may not 'take' evenly when you apply the first strokes. If this happens, leave the paint to dry and apply further coats to build up the colour.

Caring for marble and stone

*Stone is tough and durable with an
attractive finish that makes it a popular, though
expensive, choice for surfaces and
ornaments in the home. To keep it looking its best, it
needs careful handling and special cleaning.*

Marble

The most familiar of decorative
household stones, marble, is a form
of limestone. Most marble is veined
by impurities which give it the dis-
tinct mottled appearance. It comes
in a range of colours, including
white veined with grey, black, red,
brown, pink, and yellow.

The Victorians were particularly
fond of marble and used it in the
home for fireplaces, larder shelves,
table tops and washstand tops.
Today it is also made into lamp
bases, cheeseboards and ashtrays
amongst other items. Its cool surface is ideal for rolling out pastry.

However, marble is not ideal for
general kitchen use as it stains
easily with many common kitchen
ingredients, such as fruit juice,
blood and fish juices. While it is

△ *Cool marble surfaces add a touch
of style to a home and are
extremely hard wearing.*

durable, marble is also semi-porous
and to protect the surface and
bring out its beauty, a wax finish
can be applied. If stains penetrate
this polished surface they can be
difficult to remove.

Regular cleaning of marble

Use soap flakes (not detergent) dissolved in warm water with a few drops of ammonia added. Rinse the surface well, then dry.

Removing stains from marble

On marks or dried stains use a mild abrasive (see fruit juices), rinse, then dry. If a piece of marble is badly stained, treat with a proprietary marble cleaner, following the manufacturer's instructions. For specific stains, follow the instructions below.

Grease stains

These can seep into the marble without actually damaging the surface. To remove the stain, the grease must be drawn out of the pores.

You will need

◇ Acetone or white spirit
◇ Lint-free cloth
◇ White blotting paper
◇ Acid-free tape

1 Dab the stain with a lint-free cloth moistened in acetone or white spirit. This should lift the grease out of the marble. If this does not remove the mark, proceed to step 2.

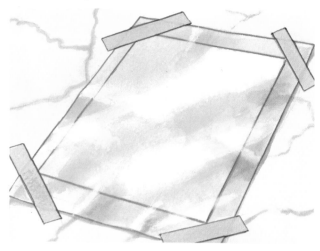

2 Soak the blotting paper in white spirit or acetone and lay over the mark. Cover the area with a sheet of plastic and tape in place to keep out the air and stop the paper from drying out. Leave it to work on the stain for about one hour.

3 Remove the cover and check the stain. If it is still there repeat the procedure several times if necessary, until the grease lifts out.

Fruit juices and wine

These are acid stains that eat through the polished surface. If the stain is not deep, first try to remove it by polishing the surface. Use a mild abrasive such as French chalk, pumice powder or tin oxide. Apply the abrasive powder with a cloth, rubbing in a circular motion. When the stain has disappeared and the area feels smooth, rinse and dry the surface.

Tea and coffee stains

Used mugs and glasses should be kept well away from marble surfaces as they can leave ring marks that discolour the stone. Ring marks can be removed with a weak borax solution made of 2tsp borax to $\frac{1}{2}$ pint (300ml) warm water. Use a cloth to rub this over the mark. Wipe clean with a cloth rinsed in clean water.

Pale marble surfaces with dark stains may need to be treated with a weak bleach solution made of one part 20-volume hydrogen peroxide to two parts water. Make sure the surface to be treated is flat and steady by propping up any sides which are rocky.

Pour the solution on to the stain and add a few drops of ammonia. When the peroxide starts to bubble, rinse immediately with clear water. Rinse again, then dry well. Repeat if necessary.

Yellowed polish

Wash with a solution of detergent and warm water, immersing the item if possible. If yellowing remains, dab on a solution of hydrogen peroxide and ammonia (see tea and coffee stains). Rinse well.

Re-sealing with wax

Apply a special marble sealer or silicone wax to the surface. Do not use wax furniture polish, as the tint can stain the surface. Just before the wax is dry, dust the surface with white talcum powder. This will fill the pores, keeping out dust and grime.

For a high shine, buff up with an electric drill fitted with a lambswool polishing pad.

Surface repairs

Any valuable item, no matter how slight the damage, should always be repaired and restored by an expert.

Chips

Marble chips fairly easily at the edges. If an item is not valuable, fill cracks or holes with a mixture of adhesive and talcum powder. Use food colouring to tint the dye to match the stone — there is then no health hazard if the dye seeps out of the adhesive.

You will need

◇ Coarse and fine glass paper
◇ White spirit
◇ Epoxy resin adhesive
◇ Talcum powder
◇ Small flexible filler knife
◇ Vegetable dye

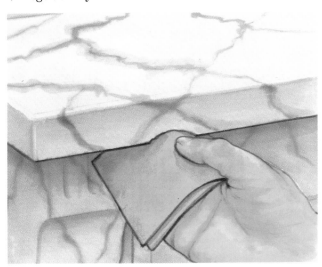

1 Using coarse glass paper, sand the chipped area, then clean well with white spirit. Leave to dry.

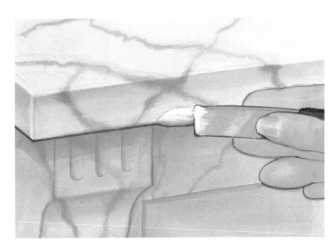

2 Mix the epoxy resin with a little talcum powder and food colouring until a close colour match is reached and it looks opaque. Fill the chip so that the mixture is just higher than surrounding surface. Leave to harden.

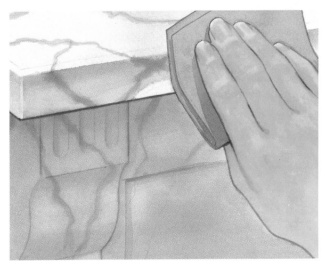

3 Sand with fine glass paper until the filled area is flush with the rest of the surface.

Scratches

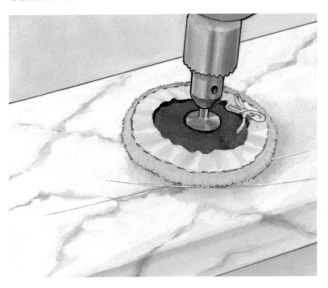

Fine scratches can be removed using abrasive powder (French chalk or putty powder) and a buffing attachment on an electric drill. Deep scratches need to be treated by an expert.

Alabaster

Alabaster is a form of gypsum. It is a translucent stone and looks similar to marble but has no veins. It can be white, cream or tones of yellow. It is absorbent and soft and is often carved into ornaments, lamp bases and sculptures.

Regular care Modern alabaster is usually fragile and easily damaged, so handle it with care. It is soluble in water so never clean it with water or soak it.

To clean Apply white spirit with a soft brush or rag and wipe dry.

To remove stains Moisten a rag in turpentine then dip in powdered pumice. Rub stain until it disappears, then clean as above.

Granite

This is an expensive, but popular, material for kitchen work surfaces and is ideal for this purpose. Most granite is very hard, difficult to damage and easy to keep clean.

Choose carefully when buying granite for worktops. Some granites are prone to cracking because of faults in the structure, while others can be porous.

Stains may not show up, but if liquids are absorbed the surface will become unhygienic.

Regular care Good quality granite needs little cleaning. Simply wipe regularly with water and mild detergent, then wipe dry.

Onyx

True onyx is a precious stone and too expensive for general use. Most 'onyx' in the home — often used for table tops and ornaments — is in fact a green mottled or veined marble-like stone.

Regular care As for marble.

△ Stone will last for years if properly maintained. From kitchen to bathroom it adds charm while being extremely hard wearing.

Soapstone

Soapstone is a very soft stone formed from magnesium and china clay. It has a mottled, opaque appearance and can be soft pink, beige or yellow. It is often made into intricately carved ornaments.

Regular care Soapstone needs careful handling as it can be easily scratched. Wash gently with soapy water and a soft brush.

To obtain a sheen Rub with a very fine abrasive such as putty powder or jeweller's rouge.

◁ Stone table tops combine function with decorative effect but take care not to rest wet objects on them. Rim marks look ugly and can be difficult to remove.

Slate

This stone consists mainly of aluminium silicate. It is extremely hard and durable and is used for fireplaces and hearths, floors, place mats and ornaments.

It can be pale to dark grey, and earthy green and red. Its surface can be polished smooth or used with a rough, riven texture.

Regular care Scrub with a solution of detergent and water, then rinse and dry.

Remove sooty fireplace or hearth stains with a mild bleach solution or proprietary stone cleaner, then rinse and dry.

To revive dull polished stone, apply linseed oil very sparingly with a soft cloth.

Restoring ironwork

*Many houses have ornamental ironwork outdoors,
usually in the form of railings, gates, balconies, and furniture. Sadly,
iron is prone to rust unless it is well protected
with paint or some other surface finish, but some straightforward
restoration work can soon put things right.*

Cast iron, wrought iron and mild steel are the main metals used for outdoor ornamental ironwork. All these metals have a common enemy, rust, which forms on the metal surface due to the combined action of water, oxygen and carbon dioxide.

Apart from making metalwork look shabby, if left untreated rust can eventually corrode right through the component it has attacked.

Renovating ironwork is a dirty, messy job but the results make a stunning difference to the front of a house, patio or item of furniture.

Preparation

Work on a fine, still day and spread a dust sheet or newspaper underneath and around the work area to contain the mess and prevent paths or floors becoming marked with paint splashes.

Wear old clothes or overalls and protect your hands with heavy-duty fabric gloves. Goggles should be worn at all times when removing rust and when spray painting.

Work away from the house where possible to prevent dust particles and paint fumes drifting indoors.

33

Removing rust

Rust should be treated as soon as it develops to prevent permanent damage to the metal. Never paint over rust, as it will continue to eat away at the metal under the paint.

The first step is to strip off all the paint, using a proprietary paint stripper. Hot air guns or blowlamps are not very effective for stripping paint from ironwork because the metal conducts heat away from the surface very quickly. With cast iron, the metal may crack under localized heating.

Then, all traces of rust must be scoured away. Rub off light deposits with wet-and-dry abrasive paper or use a proprietary rust remover. With deep, extensive rusting either hire a wire wheel or cup brush on an electric drill, or use a wire brush and plenty of elbow grease.

A proprietary rust inhibitor should then be painted on to the exposed metal. Traditional red lead, calcium plumbate or lead-free zinc phosphate primer can be bought at most car accessory and DIY shops.

For the top coat, use solvent-based gloss or eggshell paint. Do not use water-based paints as these will give fresh rust a head start.

In most cases paint has to be brushed on. Use a brush that matches the width of the metalwork to be painted. Take care to avoid runs and paint build-up on edges.

Alternatively, use aerosol paint or, for large jobs, hire a spray gun. Spray painting is ideal for items such as garden furniture, but less useful for pieces that cannot be moved, such as railings or balconies.

Treating rust
You will need

◇ Dust sheet or newspaper
◇ Electric drill with wire wheel or cup brush head attachment
◇ Wire brush
◇ Chemical paint stripper
◇ Paint scraper or old knife
◇ Two clean cloths
◇ Rust inhibitor
◇ Paint brushes
◇ White spirit
◇ Solvent based gloss, eggshell or aerosol paint.
◇ Spray gun

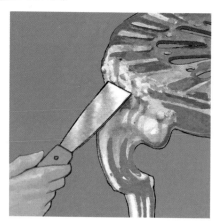

1 Place dust sheet or newspaper under and around items to be treated. Apply the paint stripper carefully following the manufacturer's instructions. Leave on until the paint bubbles and flakes. Scrape off using a paint scraper or old knife. Clean down surface according to instructions.

▽ *Well maintained wrought iron furniture adds elegance and charm to a garden or patio.*

2 Use the electric drill with a wire wheel to remove the rust. Finish awkward crevices with a wire brush. Sweep away any loose bits with a soft brush.

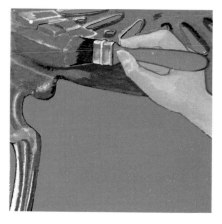

3 Dust the surface with a clean dry cloth. Apply a proprietary rust inhibitor following the manufacturer's instructions.

4 Degrease the surface thoroughly by wiping with white spirit. Apply metal primer as soon as the spirit has evaporated. Give edges and corners a generous coat for added protection.

5 When the primer is thoroughly dry, apply the top coat using a spray gun, moving the gun with an even sweep.

Repairs to cupboards

Cupboard doors and drawers work hard for a living
so small but irritating faults can occur in their usually smooth
running. Here some common problems and their
remedies are covered. Often a simple repair job can considerably
increase ease of use, good looks and efficiency.

Repairing doors

The two main causes of ill fitting cupboard doors are faulty hinges and warping of the door wood. With a screwdriver, hammer and plane these problems can soon be taken care of.

Hinges

Hinges are a regular source of trouble. With constant use screws become loose, causing doors to stick and drop out of line. Familiarity with the different types of hinges makes identifying and solving the problem much easier.

Butt hinges are used widely on wooden doors and found particularly on older cupboard doors. The hinge plates need to be fitted into recesses cut into the door and door frame.

From the outside, the spine of the hinge will be visible where the door joins the cupboard. A gap appears between the two sides when the door is opened.

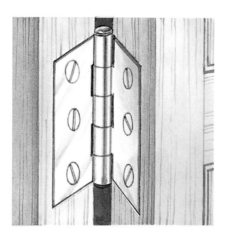

Concealed hinges are used on most modern furniture, particularly kitchen units, wardrobes and cupboards which have surface-mounted doors. They are invisible from the outside and are easy to adjust when a door drops out of line.

There are two types. Lay-on concealed hinges are simply screwed to the door and the side of the cabinet and do not need to be recessed. This makes them easier to fit if you have to replace them, but they are more obvious when the door is open than the recessed type. The latter are more popular as they give a neater finish and are easier to adjust if a door drops out of line.

Adjusting a concealed hinge

When a door drops out of line, it becomes difficult to close and often catches on the door next to it. If the doors have set-in concealed hinges, the offending door can soon be manoeuvred back into line.

These hinges are specially made to make them easy to adjust. The hinge mechanism is recessed into the back of the door. The arm attached to this slots into a baseplate on the inside of the cabinet. This arm can be adjusted by loosening the appropriate screw to realign the door. In the following diagrams, the screw to be loosened is indicated by pink shading. Remember to use a screwdriver that matches the hinge screws.

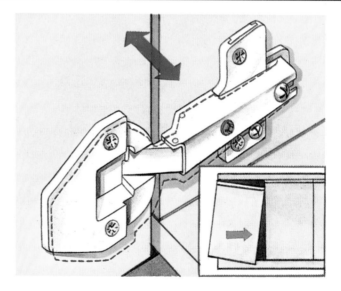

On a door that has slipped down at one corner
Loosen the screw indicated in the diagram. Move the door back into its correct position by rocking it sideways, then re-tighten the screw.

Repairs to cupboard doors
Faults on traditional timber doors
A squeaking door may be due to one of two causes. The metal hinges may simply need oiling, or the door may be catching on the frame as it opens and shuts.

Oiling
Use the household oil on the hinge. Hold a cloth under the hinge to catch any drips and apply a drop at a time. Leave the oil to soak in well, then check if this has cured the noise.

If the door still squeaks and the hinge is very stiff, remove it and apply a penetrating oil. Work the hinge until it moves easily and replace on door.

Changing a hinge

The easiest method of replacing a hinge is to remove the present hinge, and then take it with you to buy an identical new one so that recess and screw holes remain in the same place.

All you then need to do is to screw the new hinge in position. You may need to pack out the screw holes as described below to make sure the new screws hold firmly.

If you want to replace a hinge with a new design, the easiest to fit are lay-on hinges, as no recess has to be cut. To fit a set-in hinge a circular hole has to be drilled. A special drill bit called a hinge sinker is used to do this. Choose one to match the size of hole needed for the new hinge.

Concealed hinges vary in the degree to which they open. You may find you want to open a door further, so this would be a good time to get a wider angled hinge.

Repairing hinges
Loose screws

Constant wear can loosen a screw. To tighten it use the same type of screwdriver as screw — single-slot or cross-head — in the nearest size to the screw head. The wrong size of screwdriver can damage both screwdriver and screw. This may only be a temporary repair as the screw hole often becomes enlarged so that the screw is no longer a tight fit. In this case the hole will need packing out with matchsticks or dowelling so that the screw can bite into the material again.

Packing out a screw hole

If the hole is only slightly larger than the screw it can be packed out with matchsticks. Cut matchstick lengths to the depth of the hole then pack the hole tightly with them, lightly tapping the sticks well into the hole with a hammer. Finally replace the screw.

For a more efficient long term method enlarge the hole with a drill bit then fit a length of dowelling into it. Cut the dowelling to fit the hole length, which should be slightly longer than the screw length. Use wood glue to coat both hole and dowel then tap the dowel into the hole. When the glue is dry refit the hinge with a new screw.

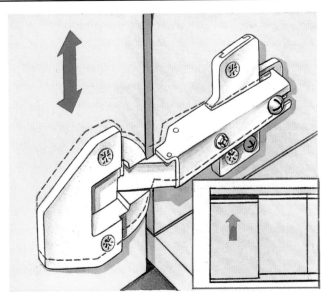

On a door that has dropped loosen the screw indicated in the diagram. Push the door and hinge plate up into position. Hold in place as you tighten the screw.

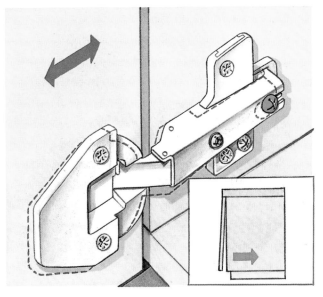

To move the door in or out loosen the screw indicated in the diagram. Adjust by sliding the hinge in or out to match adjoining doors, then refit the screw.

Catching door

If a door is catching on the frame, the first thing to do is to find the problem spot.

To do this, place a strip of carbon paper between the frame and door in the area where the problem is occurring. Shut the door, with the carbon in between. The carbon will leave a mark in the spot where the trouble is being caused.

Small protrusions can be sanded back easily using coarse then fine sandpaper. Larger areas will need planing. Remove a thin sliver of wood and check the fit. If it is still catching, remove a little more wood. Continue planing and checking until the door once more closes with ease.

Padding out hinge rebate

The door may be catching on the hinge side because the butt hinges are set too deep in the rebates. With some small pieces of hinge card and a screwdriver (which matches the hinge screws), this is fixed quite easily.

1 Unscrew the hinge on the faulty side. Use it as a template to cut rectangles from the card.

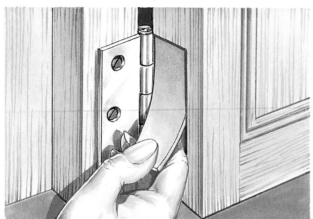

2 Pack out hinge recess with the card until hinge sits flush with surrounding surface. Screw hinge back in place.

Realigning a warped door

A door warped on the hinge side can usually be mended by adding another hinge to pull it into position.

Warping on the opening side can be put right by forcing the door back into its correct position and holding it there. In time it will be pulled back permanently into its original shape. Again few tools and materials are needed; a hammer and screwdriver, some thin strips of wood and possibly a couple of bolts should do the job.

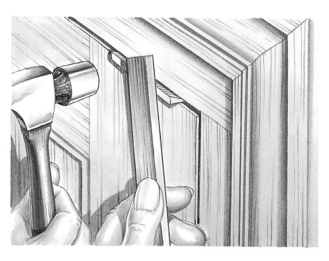

For a door sticking at the top or bottom, force the door back into position (down for the top, up for the bottom) then carefully hammer thin wedges of wood in the slit to hold it in place. Do the same for a door sticking at the side, but insert the wedge half way down the side to hold it.

When hammering the strips of wood into place, use another strip between hammer and wedge to protect the cupboard surface.

Repairs to drawers
Modern unit drawers

These usually move in and out on metal or plastic runners. If any part of the roller mechanism or the runners become damaged they will need to be replaced with new. In most cases the drawer is removed by opening it wide and lifting the front, then back off the runners. Remove the faulty section and take it to a stockist to order a replacement part. Fit the new part in the same way that you removed the faulty one.

Traditional timber drawers

A sticking drawer may simply need sanding lightly and lubricating. The drawers in older timber furniture run on wooden runners. Try sandpapering the drawer sides and lubricating the runners by rubbing with candle wax; this may be all that is needed to make them run smoothly again.

With constant use the runners can become worn, making the drawer loose or awkward as it runs over the damaged spot. A worn runner will need to be removed and replaced with a matching length of wood. Glue then pin each new runner to hold it in place.

Sometimes the base of a drawer that has been over filled may bow or become broken. These usually run in grooves in the drawer sides and are easily removed and replaced with a new piece of plywood cut to fit.

Fitting new handles

The simplest way to give a kitchen a new look is to replace ugly handles. Choose a design that fits in with the design of the furniture and, if possible, will fit into the same holes as the old handles. Remove an old handle and take it with you when buying replacements so that you can check this. Otherwise you will need to fill the original holes and stain or paint the filling to match the furniture, before drilling new holes to take the new handles.

▽ *Doors and drawers which fit properly look neat and help to make life about the house much easier.*

Renovating furniture

*New furniture is expensive to buy, particularly
if you want something a bit different. Yet junk shops are
teeming with inexpensive pieces of furniture
which, with a bit of thought and handiwork, can be turned into
an original centre-piece for a room.*

The shabby chest of drawers (top right) was found in a junk shop. The frame was basically sound and after the few repairs described in the following pages, was ready for decorating. The subtle colours and light details bring out a rustic character in the piece.

Browsing round second-hand furniture shops will turn up unexpected treasures waiting to be given a new lease of life. Each piece of furniture will have its own problems and these need to be assessed before the item is purchased, to make sure that the repairs needed are not too time consuming or difficult to do.

This chapter concentrates on renovating a chest of drawers and a washstand. It explains how to repair common problems associated with these two items of furniture in general, such as broken drawers and doors, missing castors and warped cupboard bases. Many of these tips can be applied to other furniture.

Once the piece of furniture has been repaired, the pleasurable task of decorating the exterior can begin. The item can be decorated to co-ordinate with the decor of a room or alternatively the character of the piece itself can provide the inspiration for the decoration. Whichever direction you take, the final result will be a personalized item of furniture — for a fraction of the cost of buying the same item new.

Chest of drawers

Drawers are constantly in use and tend to suffer the worst damage. Badly worn runners, missing drawer stops and warped or loose drawer bases are the usual problems. Missing or loose handles and knobs are another problem.

Once mended, the chest can be stripped back and varnished; waxed to bring out the grain of the wood, or painted. (For detailed advice on how to strip, varnish and wax pieces of furniture, see pages 43-52.)

Repairing runners

Runners often develop grooves making it hard to move the drawers. These runners are either the sides of the drawer which extend down $\frac{1}{2}$in (6mm) below the drawer base or strips placed inside the frame of the chest. In both cases the wood needs to be levelled off and a piece of wood added to build it up to its original height.

Match the original runner when buying the extra wood. This may only need to be between $\frac{1}{8}$ to $\frac{1}{4}$in thick. A joinery or DIY shop should be able to cut the timber to the correct dimensions for you.

Do not nail the extra piece in place or the nail heads will catch on the drawer. Instead, stick firmly with a strong wood adhesive.

Mending a drawer runner

The entire runner will need to be planed down so that it is level and a new strip added to bring it back to the original depth.

You will need
◇ Plane
◇ Saw
◇ Wood strip
◇ Adhesive
◇ 'G' cramp
◇ Fine glass paper
◇ Furniture wax
◇ 0000 wire wool

1 Measure the height of the runner at an undamaged point. Plane down the runner until it is level and measure the height of the runner again. Subtract this figure from the original one to calculate how much has to be added to the runner.

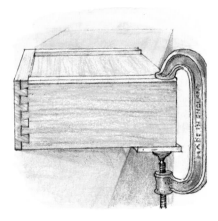

2 If necessary, trim the strip of wood so that it is the same width as the existing runner, then cut it to the same length as the side of the drawer. Plane the strip so that it is the depth needed to build up the runner (the final measurement noted in step 1). Glue and clamp strip on top of the existing runner. Wipe off any excess glue with a damp cloth. Leave to dry with clamp in place.

3 Remove clamp and sand down the runner with a fine grade glass paper. Wipe away dust. Apply wax using fine wire wool.

Mending a chest runner

Only the damaged area needs to be cut out and replaced with a sound piece of wood. This must be levelled to the same height as the runner or the drawer will catch.

You will need
The materials listed above plus:
◇ Chisel
◇ Sandpaper

1 Chisel out the damaged area forming a straight sided gap. Sand smooth with sandpaper followed by fine glass paper.

2 Measure height, depth and width of gap. Mark out dimensions on a piece of wood and cut out shape. Make the shape larger, rather than smaller, as it is easier to reduce the wood to the right size.

3 Try the piece for size, and alter if necessary. Glue and clamp in place. Leave to dry.

4 Remove clamp. Sand down the top to ensure it is even with the runner. Wax as given before.

Replacing drawer stops

These are small pieces of wood stuck to the front rail to prevent the drawer from being pushed into the back of the chest of drawers. They are often missing but can be replaced with scraps of wood.

The replacement pieces must be positioned correctly on the rail or the drawer will not line up with the front. Drawers may have one or two stops. The outline of the old stop may be visible on the rail making it easy to position the new one.

You will need
◇ Scrap of wood
◇ Marker and ruler
◇ Dovetail saw
◇ Sandpaper
◇ Adhesive
◇ Finishing pins
◇ Hammer
◇ Tape measure

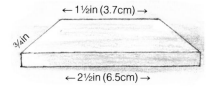

← 1½in (3.7cm) →
¾in
← 2½in (6.5cm) →

1 On a scrap of wood ¼in (6mm), mark out a shape 2½in (6.5cm) at the front, 1½in (3.8cm) at the back and ¾in (2cm) at the sides. Cut out using a dovetail saw. Sand edges to make them smooth.

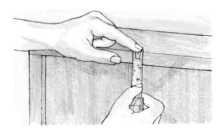

2 Measure the depth of the drawer front. Measure the same amount in from the front edge of the rail. Draw a horizontal line across the rail at this point.

3 Position longer edge of drawer stop along this line. Glue and pin in place. Wipe away excess glue. Leave to dry.

Repairing a drawer base

The drawer base is usually fitted into a slot at the front of the drawer and fixed to the back with nails or screws. Often the base will shrink in dry conditions, causing it to pull out of the front slot. This can be mended by simply removing the fastening at the back, sliding the base back into the groove and re-fastening it.

Making a new drawer base

If the drawer base is very badly damaged it will have to be replaced. Use either plywood or a wooden panel for this, depending on the original material used. The size of the panel will be the same as the inside of the drawer plus an allowance for the side and front slots. The panel should be a fraction under the thickness of the slots — usually about ¼in (6mm). Plywood of the correct thickness can be bought from DIY stores. A solid wooden panel can be bought from a joinery shop where they will cut it to size for you. The grain of the solid wooden panel should run from side to side.

You will need
◇ Saw
◇ Tape measure
◇ Marker
◇ Set square and ruler
◇ Sandpaper
◇ Hammer or screwdriver

1 Remove the damaged drawer base. Turn the drawer upside down and measure round the inside edges. Push the end of the tape measure into the grooves to measure their depth. Add groove measurements to relevant sides.

2 On the replacement plywood, mark out the base outline. Use a set square to make sure the corners are at 90°. Cut out the shape with a saw. Sand down the rough edges.

3 Slide the new base into place and secure in position at the back with nails or screws.

Replacing handles

Sometimes handles or knobs are missing from drawers. It may be possible to find a close match from furniture restoration shops or by taking one from a piece of furniture which is beyond repair.

Alternatively, replace all of the knobs or handles with a new set. When replacing handles with knobs, or when altering the positioning of handles, the old holes will have to be filled. If the chest is to be varnished or waxed, fill the holes with a tinted wood filler close to the colour of wood. If the chest is to be painted, white wood stopping can be used.

You will need
◇ Wood filler
◇ Spatula
◇ Fine glass paper
◇ Yardstick and pencil
◇ Drill
◇ Knobs

1 Remove the old handles. Fill the holes with wood filler. Leave to set. A second application of filler may be needed if the holes are large. Sand filler level with drawer surface.

2 To find centre of the drawer, lightly mark diagonal lines from each corner. The centre is the point where these diagonals cross. If using handles, position holes equal distance from centre point and parallel to drawer base.

3 Use a drill bit slightly larger than the diameter of the screw or screws holding the handle. Drill a hole at the centre point if adding knobs, making sure to drill straight into the wood. Drill holes as marked for handles. Sand away frayed edges. Screw the knobs or handles in place.

Washstand

This washstand needed some simple repairs to make it functional — repairs that are likely to occur on other washstands. It was imaginatively decorated, to make it a very desirable item of furniture.

Repairing the door

Often the door may not hang properly. To correct this problem, re-tighten the hinge screws. Check for paint build-up and, if it exists, rub it away with coarse abrasive paper, then a finer paper.

Polishing the marble

The beautiful marble top had become marked and dull. The marks were treated and the surface well polished following the instructions given on pages 29-31.

◁ ▽ *Although badly battered, this washstand obviously had a lovely marble top and elegant front. Quite a lot of work was needed to make the frame sound. The door, base, legs and top needed attention. The upstand (upright piece on top) was beyond repair so a new one was made. Rather than use tiles to decorate this, a shaped panel was added. This was then painted with the motif carved on the front panels. Light, pastel shades were used to contrast with the dark marble and give a bright, fresh piece of bathroom furniture.*

Repairing the base

In the washstand shown, the supports for the base of the cupboard had come unglued. To repair similar damage: wash or prise away the old glue. Lightly sand the old supports. Re-glue the old supports and clamp them in place while the glue dries. Re-attach the base with finishing pins.

Replacing the upstand

The upstand was beyond repair so a new one was made. MDF board was used for the replacement as it is easy to cut and paint. The new panel was cut to the measurements of the old upstand but details were added to echo the pattern in the front relief carving. New supports were also cut from MDF. The pieces were painted then glued in place. Holes were pre-drilled in upstand base in line with those in the marble top before it was bolted in place.

Replacing a castor

A missing castor will make a washstand very unstable. If the base of the leg is sound, and not split, simply replace the castor. Take one of the remaining castors to the hardware store when buying the replacement to ensure it matches. Re-insert the castors into the hole in the bottom of each leg.

The remaining castors of this washstand were rusty and stiff. To correct a similar problem, spray the castors liberally with WD-40, then rub them down with a fine wire wool to remove the rust. Rub them down again with a clean, dry rag and apply a second coat of WD-40.

Stripping wooden furniture

*Stripping old furniture is one of the
more messy aspects of renovation, but the satisfaction of
revealing the natural grain of the wood hidden
for decades beneath layers of dirty paint or darkened varnish
makes all the effort worthwhile.*

Old wooden furniture often suffers many indignities in the name of fashion; simple pieces may have been covered in thick layers of paint, badly applied varnish or topped with plastic laminate in an endeavour to 'modernize' them.

With the original wood covered in such finishes it may be difficult to believe that the furniture is worth salvaging, but with a little work most pieces can be restored. The finish must be stripped, whether you plan to varnish, paint, wax or polish the piece later.

1 Shave hook
2 Paint brush
3 Scraper
4 White spirit
5 Hot air gun
6 Sanding block
7 Rubber gloves
8 Small bricklayer's trowel
    (or palette knife)
9 Paste stripper
10 Liquid stripper
11 Fine grade wire wool
12 Sandpaper
13 Cloth

Before you start

Before you begin to sand and scrape, take a long hard look at your furniture. It is important to establish exactly what the finish is and to get an idea of the sort of wood underneath as these will affect the method of stripping you choose.

Most old pieces of furniture were finished with wax, oil, stain, varnish or French polish. But no two pieces are alike and you may find you have a table or chair which has accumulated several layers of paint. Wax is best cleaned off with a cloth covered with white spirit, and old stain has to be sanded away. Paint and varnish will need ·stripping with a hot air gun or chemical stripper.

Veneered furniture

Never assume that your table is made from solid wood. If you start to strip a heavily painted table or chest of drawers using any of the methods mentioned above you may discover a thin delicate veneer coming away with the paint scrapings. A veneered table must be identified as such before you begin. If it is impossible to tell through the finish, scrape away a small section of the paint on an inconspicuous part of the table with a craft knife so you can study the wood underneath. The only sure way to remove the old layers of paint and varnish without destroying the veneer is to sand them off gradually by hand. Even then, you may find the veneer is damaged.

Fixtures and fittings

If your piece of furniture has metal handles or hinges or ceramic knobs, it is essential to remove them before you begin, as they can be affected by chemical or hot air strippers. Take out any drawers and treat them separately. Old chests of drawers may be fitted with wooden knobs — these can be stripped along with the rest of the surface.

◆ TIP	MAKING A REVIVING FLUID

If your furniture has an old waxed or varnished finish that is basically sound, you can use a reviving fluid to clean and enhance the patina. Mix a solution of four parts white spirit to one part linseed oil and apply to the surface with a cloth. For carved and turned sections, apply the fluid with a soft paint brush and polish off with a cloth. This will remove the layers of dirt without destroying the old finish.

Stripping different surfaces

Stained and waxed furniture

△ *Use a sanding block to remove old stained wood.*

Furniture with a stained or waxed finish must be cleaned back to the bare wood in order to give a good, fresh finish. The best way to remove old coloured wood is to sand it away. Use a sanding block and a selection of graded sandpaper, starting with a medium grade and finishing with a fine grade. Always sand with the grain of the wood to avoid unecessary scratches. For large surfaces it is worth using an electric orbital sander, but always finish by hand. Once you have reached the natural wood, polish with fine grade wire wool to give the grain a silky finish. Wax can be removed with white spirit.

Caustic stripping

This is a commercial process which involves dipping the whole piece of furniture in a large vat of caustic soda to remove the paint, then hosing it down with water. It is quick and effective, but there are pitfalls. In addition to taking the paint off it can also dissolve any glue used and cause your piece to fall apart. Certain woods tend to take on a greyish tinge.

Companies that undertake this sort of work can be found in your local directory, but make sure that you ask their professional advice before stripping anything valuable using this method.

Painted and varnished furniture

Use either a hot air gun or chemical strippers to strip furniture with a painted or varnished finish.
Electric hot air guns are a safer version of the blowtorch (which can be tricky to use and tends to scorch the wood). They heat to a high temperature, blistering and softening the paint and varnish in their airstream until it can be scraped off with a shave hook or flat scraper. Never direct the airstream at one particular spot for too long, as this can cause slight scorching that will discolour the wood below. (Discolouration is not a problem if you plan to paint over the stripped wood.)

With soft woods such as pine there is also a danger of gouging the surface when removing the paint. Use a wide scraper held at a shallow angle to lift the paint.
Chemical strippers create a chemical reaction which softens the paint. There are three kinds — liquid, gel and paste. The liquid and gel can be applied to the surface with an old paint brush and scraped off about 30 minutes later, once the paint has softened. The surface must then be neutralized with white spirit or water (according to manufacturer's instructions) to remove all traces of the stripper. Several applications may be necessary to remove a thick build-up of paint.

Paste strippers usually come in powder form and must be mixed with water before they can be applied. After about 30 minutes the paste coating can be scored with a blunt knife and peeled away along with the old paint or varnish. These strippers are particularly suitable for carved or turned pieces.

If stripping indoors, ensure the room is well ventilated, protect your floorcovering with several layers of newspaper and keep children and animals out of the way. Wear rubber gloves while you work as the chemicals can burn your skin, and dispose of the paint or varnish scrapings carefully.

Once the furniture is completely stripped, sand thoroughly and finish by rubbing down with a fine grade wire wool.

To use a hot air gun, hold the gun approximately 6in (15cm) away from the painted or varnished surface and squeeze the trigger. As soon as the paint starts to bubble, carefully scrape it away. Repeat the process until all the paint has been removed.

To apply liquid or gel stripper, stipple it on to the painted or varnished surface. When it begins to blister, remove with a scraper (use a shave hook for crevices), then scrub with water or white spirit as instructed to neutralize. Leave to dry, then sand.

When using paste stripper mix up the paste according to the manufacturer's instructions and apply with a trowel. Leave for the suggested amount of time then score the surface of the paste and peel away in strips. Scrub with clear water to neutralize.

Dealing with blemishes

Once your furniture has been stripped back to the natural wood, you may find the surface covered with small scratches, stains and blemishes. These must be dealt with before you start to apply the finish.

Woodworm

Treated insect holes can be filled with a proprietary filler. Use a palette knife for holes on flat surfaces, or a cloth to smooth it in to holes on turned sections. Leave to harden and sand smooth.

Ink stains

These are common on tables and old wooden desks. Sand the stain as much as possible, then bleach the area using oxalic acid crystals (available from pharmacists). Dissolve a tablespoon of crystals in two tablespoons of boiling water and apply with a pad of cotton wool. Leave for a few minutes, then remove. Repeat if necessary. Alternatively, use a proprietary two-part bleach following the manufacturer's instructions.

Scratches

Small scratches can be filled with coloured furniture crayon (available from hardware stores in a range of colours). Run the crayon along the line of your scratch to work it into the groove, then rub a clean cloth across the top to remove any excess and create a smooth, flat surface.

Burns

Sand away the burned wood with a piece of fine grade sandpaper wrapped around the end of a pencil, then apply a little bleach to the darkened hollow with a cotton bud. A small area can be filled with furniture crayon, but a large area is best left and treated in the same way as the rest of the surface.

Dents

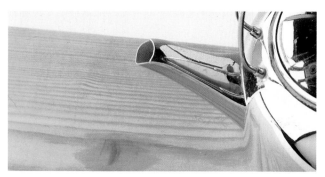

Dents can be repaired using boiling water. Apply a few drops from a kettle to the dented area to swell the wood fibres. Allow the wood to dry completely before polishing.

Cracks and splits

A proprietary wood filler should be used to fill any cracks or splits. Apply with a palette knife, working it well into the grooves, then allow to harden. Sand smooth and level with the surface.

Applying polyurethane varnish

*Once your wooden furniture has been
carefully stripped and sanded smooth, you can apply the
finish. In this introduction to the techniques
of wood finishing, we explain how to apply a durable
finish of polyurethane varnish.*

▽ *This shabby chair (inset) was stripped and then varnished
to bring out the mellow tones of the wood.*

Stripped wooden furniture can be finished in a variety of ways. The finish you choose should depend not only on the final look you are after, but the durability of the surface it provides. Any item of furniture that is subject to a lot of wear and tear, such as a kitchen chair or table, should be treated with a hardwearing finish to seal and protect the wooden surface.

One of the most durable and easy-to-apply finishes is polyurethane varnish. This can be clear or tinted to simulate real wood finishes. When applied, it creates a tough, hardwearing surface on top of the wood which needs no more than an occasional dust and can be wiped clean with a damp cloth when necessary. Coloured varnishes are also available.

Materials and equipment

Polyurethane varnish
Clear, interior, polyurethane varnish is available in gloss, silk or matt finish. It will deepen and yellow the colour of the wood considerably — if you are concerned about the final shade, test a small amount on the underside or back of your piece of furniture. Coloured polyurethane varnish builds up to give a stronger tone with every coat. For an even application (and to avoid the problem of the more absorbent end grain becoming darker) use clear varnish for the first coat to act as a sealer.

For deep penetration, polyurethane varnish can be thinned ten per cent with white spirit — this is optional but can make application easier.

Brushes
Use a new paint brush, and give it a good flick beforehand to shake off any loose bristles and dust. Keep the brush for varnish — do not use brushes which have been used to apply emulsion or gloss paint as they are certain to harbour flecks of paint.

Clean rags
A lint free rag (such as old cotton or linen sheeting, or an old handkerchief) which will not loose any fluff, is useful in two ways. It can be soaked in white spirit and wiped over bare wood to lift all traces of dust from the surface to be varnished (known as a tack rag). It will hold the dust without raising the grain of the wood, as a cloth soaked in water would.

Cotton or linen rags can also be used to apply coats of varnish evenly.

TIP	USING A CLOTH PAD

Lint free cloth pads make a good alternative to a paint brush when applying varnish, particularly for large flat surfaces. Decant the varnish into a large shallow container, such as an old aluminium freezer container, and dilute with white spirit if necessary. Fold the cloth into a small flat pad.

Dip the pad into the varnish; apply it working in a circular motion over the surface of the wood. This method makes it easier to ensure an even application.

Varnishing a chair

Once your piece of furniture has been stripped, sanded and buffed with fine grade wire wool, you can apply the varnish. Work in a light, warm, well-ventilated room, covering the floor with newspaper to protect the floorcovering from stray specks and spillages. Avoid sweeping the area beforehand, as this could raise dust which takes a while to settle and could spoil the varnished surface.

You will need
◇ Interior polyurethane varnish
◇ Jam jar or tin
◇ Clean paint brush
◇ Soft, lint free rag
◇ Fine grade wire wool or glasspaper
◇ White spirit
◇ Newspaper

1 Cover the floor with newspaper. Wipe the surface with a rag soaked in white spirit to ensure that there are no remaining specks of sawdust. Open the tin, taking great care not to shake or stir it as this causes bubbles which will affect the surface. Apply the first coat with a paint brush. You can use it straight from the tin, or thin it first with white spirit to help give a more even application.

2 Leave to dry for up to six hours. Rub lightly over the surface with fine grade wire wool or fine glasspaper to remove any accidental runs or visible brush strokes.

3 Wipe down the surface with a tack rag again, then apply the second coat of varnish and leave to dry. If necessary, apply a third, and even a fourth, coat in the same way.

4 For a more mellow effect, burnish the surface by rubbing evenly over the surface with fine grade wire wool, using a little wax polish as a lubricant. Finally, buff with a soft cloth. Clean the brush in white spirit.

Waxing and oiling

For centuries, waxes and oils have been used to protect the surface of wooden furniture. In time, the soft, lustrous finish becomes dull and may be stained or ingrained with dirt. But most stains can be successfully removed and the finish revived or totally renewed.

Surface protection

Wood surfaces can be protected and enhanced by a range of traditional finishes. The oldest wood finishes are the soft finishes, oil and wax. Hard finishes are French polish, shellac, varnishes and lacquers.

Once widely used by furniture makers, oil and wax give a lustrous sheen — unlike the high gloss of French polish – and help to protect the wood from dirt and dust. However, they can become dull and need to be revived or restored. The next few pages show how to restore a wax or oiled surface — French polish is dealt with later.

Wax polish

Wax was used long before the introduction of French polish. It is laborious to apply, but gives a beautiful finish and is easy to maintain. The surface can be marked by heat and water and soils easily. The natural base can be beeswax, carnauba wax or paraffin wax.

Beeswax comes from honeycomb and is relatively soft and slightly tacky. It provides a slight sheen.

Carnauba wax comes from palm leaves, smells like new mown hay and is harder than beeswax. It produces a tough and long lasting, more glossy finish. It is expensive and is often mixed with beeswax.

Paraffin wax, which comes from petroleum, is softer and is often the base for cheaper polishes. It is sometimes included in more expensive polishes to soften them and make them easier to apply.

Oils

A traditional oiled finish is very tough, standing up well to hot plates and mugs, spilled liquids and scratches. However, it takes a long time to build up a durable surface — layer after layer of oil is rubbed on until a soft sheen is produced. The surface is left to dry between each coat — the longer it is left to dry, the tougher the final finish.

Linseed oil, either raw or boiled, is traditionally used. Raw linseed oil takes about three days to dry, but when boiled with other substances it takes about 24 hours.

Teak or Danish oil take about four hours to dry. Teak oil produces a higher sheen than Danish oil.

Restoring a dull finish

Always check to see if you can revive the present finish — in most cases, there is no need to completely strip a piece of furniture. Remember, it is the build-up of dirt and polish, known as the patina, that gives old furniture its character.

Revivers can be purchased from hardware shops. Alternatively, make your own. Mix equal parts — about an eggcupfull — raw linseed oil and white spirit with a dash of vinegar. Put this mixture in a bottle and shake well. Apply the reviver with a soft cloth, working in circular movements. Use a new section of the cloth as the dirt lifts on to it and continue until no more dirt can be removed. On carved sections or awkward corners use a toothbrush.

For stubborn dirt which will not come off on the cloth, use very fine, 0000 grade steel wool. Work with light pressure at first in a circular motion, then apply heavier pressure if necessary. To finish off, rub lightly with the grain. Replace the pad of steel wool as it becomes clogged.

Removing the finish

If you decide to completely remove the old finish, use a spirit-based stripper. Choose one that is washed down with methylated spirit or white spirit, rather than water.

Do not use a water-based stripper or one that must be removed with water because water will lift the grain of the wood. Check the instructions on the can or bottle before buying.

Follow the manufacturer's instructions for use. On good timber, remove the gravy-like deposit with 0000 grade wire wool. Never use a scraper. Wipe over with a cloth until no stain shows on the cloth. When the surface is dry repeat these steps once again.

Special equipment

Steel wool comes in five grades — No. 5 is the coarsest and 0000 is the finest. When working on fine furniture use the finest grade. Many hardware shops do not stock the finest grade — you may have to ask them to order it for you.

Removing marks and stains

Old table tops are often stained with ink, water or alcohol or have heat rings or scratches. Scratches or stains affecting only the finish of the wood are fairly easy to remove. But if a mark has gone right through the finish to the wood underneath, the finish will need to be removed and replaced.

Try the appropriate stain removal method (see also page 46). If this does not work, clean the surface with reviver. As a last resort, strip the finish and repolish.

White spots, rings or patches

You will need:

◇ White spirit
◇ 0000 grade steel wool
◇ Flour paper
◇ Metal polish

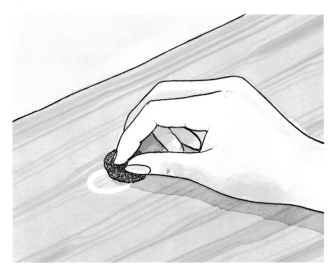

1 Dip the steel wool in white spirit. Rub it over the mark, following the grain. If the stain remains, try step 2.

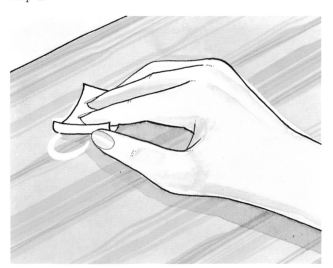

2 Dampen the stain with a little white spirit. Rub gently with flour paper following the direction of the grain. As the stain begins to lift, reapply a little white spirit and continue to rub gently.

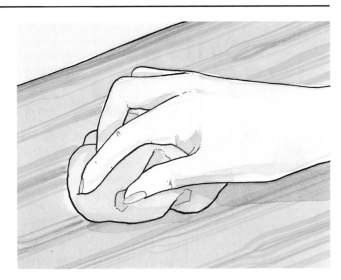

Oil finish
You will need
◇ Teak, Danish or boiled linseed oil
◇ Saucepan and jam jar for heating the oil
◇ Soft, lint-free cloth
◇ Clean rags or kitchen paper

1 Warm the oil by placing it in the jam jar in a pan of hot water. Remove the jar when the oil is warm to the touch. Do not over-heat the oil.

2 Pour oil on to the cloth and rub in well over the furniture surface. Wipe off the excess with clean rags or kitchen paper. Leave for a few days until the surface is thoroughly dry.

3 Repeat the process every few days until an attractive sheen has developed.

4 To keep the surface in good condition, periodically apply another coat of oil.

3 Finally polish the area with metal polish. Metal polish acts as a very mild abrasive, helping to clean and polish the surface.

Scratches
Scratches in the surface only can be filled. First clean out the scratch with flour paper, then fill with a matching colour wax shoe polish or wax crayon. Finish by polishing with wax polish.

Applying a new finish
If a deeper colour is required, stain the surface first. If you are oiling the wood, remember that the oil will darken the stain.

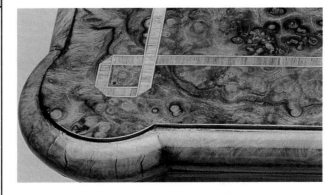

△ *A reviver was used to bring out the beauty of this fine waxed table.*

Wax polish

You will need:

◇ Clear French polish
◇ 2in (5cm) paintbrush
◇ Wax polish
◇ Shoebrush
◇ Soft, lint-free cloth
◇ Small brush for carved areas

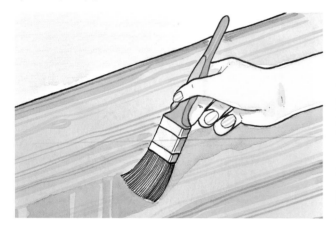

1 Clean any mouldings or carvings with white spirit. Allow to dry. Brush on a thin coat of French polish. This seals the wood so that it will not absorb the wax and dirt that may work its way through from the surface. Allow to dry and repeat.

2 When the furniture is quite dry apply a thin layer of wax polish over the surface using the cloth. Use the small brush on mouldings. Leave the wax to dry.

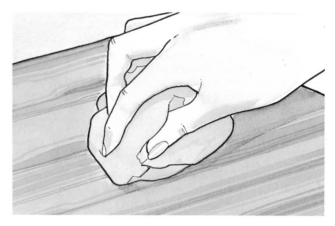

3 Polish the surface well with a shoebrush then buff with a dry cloth. Leave for a few days to harden before applying a second coat.

4 To maintain in good condition, apply a thin coat of wax about every two months. Periodically clean the surface with reviver then reapply the wax.

Home-made wax polish

You will need:

◇ 2 blocks pure beeswax
◇ Pure turpentine
◇ Grater
◇ Metal container
◇ Large bowl

3 Stir to help the beeswax dissolve, adding more hot water to the outer container if necessary. Decant the melted polish into a new tin. Keep sealed when not in use.

Safety point.
Turpentine is highly inflammable so never heat it over a flame.

1 Grate the beeswax into slivers. Place in the tin and just cover with turpentine.

2 Put the container into the bowl and pour boiling water around it. Don't get any water in the beeswax and turpentine mix.

French polishing

*French polishing gives a high shine, enhancing the
beauty of close-grained woods with a smooth and glass-like
finish. The technique is painstaking, but with
patience and practice, the amateur can renew the damaged
surface of a cherished piece of furniture.*

△ *French polishing highlights the
richness and depth of colour on a
simple Georgian mahogany table.*

▷ *The glass-like finish of French
polish enhances the beauty of this
Victorian walnut Wellington chest.*

French polish became very popular in Victorian times because of its mirror-like shine and smooth, hard surface. This finish is still popular today, but it is best for pieces which are only used with care, as it does not stand up well to heat, water or scratches. It is not suitable for any furniture in constant use.

The finish is produced, like oiling, by gradually building up the surface in stages so that the wood grain is completely filled in. The polish is applied with a rubber — a chunk of cotton wool saturated in polish and then wrapped in a cotton rag. When working, warm, dry and dust-free conditions are essential.

French polish test

French polish has a glass-like finish, without traces of brush marks or sandpaper. Heat causes white opaque marks and water can leave areas of white polish which has lost its transparent quality. Bruises and scratches may be surrounded by a flaked, yellow-white finish. To check for French polishing, drop a little methylated spirits on to the surface — the polish will soften and lose its shine.

Restoring the finish

A French polished surface can often be revived or patched up. Unless the surface is severely damaged, check to see whether a little remedial work can restore the shine before you strip off the finish.

To restore a dull finish or to remove surface stains, see page 50. However, do not follow this method to restore a dull finish on a cracked French polished surface – the oil may seep through the cracks and leave dark stains on the surface of the wood which are hard to remove afterwards.

Special materials

French polish is available from most major DIY stores. It is made from shellac and methylated spirits, with various hardeners.

Shellac comes from the secretions of an insect, the lac, which inhabits trees in India and Thailand. Various types of polish are produced from shellac.

Button polish gives bleached wood a golden tone and ordinary unstained woods an orange colour.

French polish can vary considerably in colour from pale orange to dark brown. It is suitable for use on most woods to give a medium tone.

White French polish is milky-white in colour and is made from bleached shellac. Use it to retain a pale colour on the wood.

Transparent French polish is also made from bleached shellac and is suitable for retaining the wood's natural colour.

Tinted French polish may be necessary where a piece of furniture is made of more than one wood. This may show up after the first coat of French polish is applied — use stains to tint the polish in the lighter areas to match these to the darker ones.

Preparation

French polish magnifies any imperfections in the surface of the wood so it is very important to start with a near perfect finish. After removing the old finish (see pages 44-46), look at the surface of the wood carefully.

Fill holes and bruises with plastic wood or stopping. Pick a shade to match the surrounding wood and work the filler into the dent or hole with a spatula or putty knife. When dry, sand level with the surrounding surface.

Next, the furniture may need to be re-stained to restore its original

▽ A battered old box makes an excellent first project for learning French polishing techniques.

▽ With patience and careful rubbing, the warmth of the wood is revealed in a rich, glowing surface.

colour. Test the stain colour in a hidden spot first. If necessary, mix two or more stains to obtain exactly the right shade.

The French polish will fill most of the wood's pores so it is not essential to fill the grain of the wood before starting. The wood finish does need to be smooth.

Method

Test the polish colour and practise the technique on a wood offcut before attempting a piece of furniture. Only start when confident about your technique and results. Work in a warm, dust-free room.

You will need

◇ 2 large white cotton handkerchiefs or 2 pieces of white lint-free cotton fabric about 9in (23cm) square
◇ Cotton wool
◇ French polish
◇ Methylated spirits
◇ Linseed oil
◇ Flour paper
◇ Finest glasspaper
◇ Rubber gloves
◇ Air-tight, screw-top jars for storing the rubbers

Making a rubber

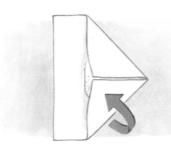

1 Pull off a piece of cotton wool big enough to fill the palm of your hand. Shape it like a pear with one flat side. Pummel cotton wool into shape and place, flat side down, in the centre of the cotton square.

2 Fold fabric over pointed end of the cotton wool, then fold one corner into the centre, trapping the first fold.

3 Fold in adjacent corner to meet the first one, trapping the other end of the first fold.

4 Twist the other corners of the cotton together to hold in place. The centre of the square forms the sole of this shoe shape. With your forefinger on the pointed end, check that the pad falls comfortably between your thumb and second finger. Adjust the pad to fit if necessary.

5 Wearing rubber gloves, open out the rubber carefully and pour French polish on to the centre of the cotton wool from the top. Use enough to just saturate it. Fold back into shape. When not in use store each rubber in its own air-tight screw-top jar.

TIP	CLEANING

◇ To clean a French polished surface, rub with a soft dry cloth. Occasionally polish with a tiny amount of furniture cream.
◇ Seek professional advice if a mark is particularly bad or you are in any way unsure about treatment.

Bodying up

1 Wearing rubber gloves, dab the pad on to a hard flat surface until the polish starts to appear on the surface from the pointed front of the rubber.

2 Slide the rubber on to the surface of the furniture and move it back and forth, following the grain. Use long, smooth, firm strokes.

3 Use fingers to squeeze the pad and control the polish flow. In this first stage the aim is to push polish into the grain to seal the wood, leaving only a thin layer on the surface.

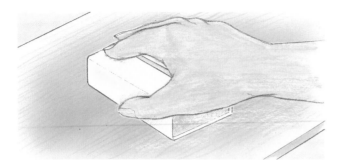

4 Increase the pressure on the rubber as the polish is used up. If the rubber sticks, add a small drop of linseed oil to the surface of the pad. Make sure that the corners and edges of the piece get as much attention as the centre.

5 When the first coat is dry (usually about 15 minutes) rub over the surface very lightly using flour paper. This removes any small particles of dirt stuck in the polish.

6 Apply a second, more sparing, coat of polish. This time use a circular movement along the surface, in parallel lines, overlapping each circle with the one behind and above (or below, depending on direction of work). Keep the pressure on the rubber the same all the time or circular lines will show up.

7 When dry rub down, apply another coat, this time using a figure of eight movement. Continue applying polish sparingly in the same way.

8 When the wood surface is completely sealed, the rubber stops sliding easily. Apply one drop only of linseed oil to the rubber base and continue applying polish.

9 When quite a lot of polish has been applied, leave the piece for 24 hours in a dust-free room.

Building up

1 The next day, rub over the surface with fine glasspaper and wipe away dust. Charge rubber with a little polish and add a small drop of linseed oil to the outside of the pad. Apply lightly, wiping it over the wood rather than rubbing it in. Start off with the grain, then against it, then rub in circular and figures of eight movements.

2 When taking the rubber off the work to inspect the piece or re-charge, glide it off the edge — never lift it straight up as this can spoil the finish.

3 When the surface is smooth and glossy, and has developed enough depth, charge the pad with a mixture of French polish and a

few drops of methylated spirits. Rub this mixture over the surface in the same way.

4 Leave to dry. Sand the surface carefully, wipe away dust, then add another bodying coat. The surface will need at least three bodying coats to achieve a smooth and glossy finish.

Finishing

Make up a new rubber. Charge with a few drops of methylated spirits — the rubber should feel cold and dry. Using circular movements and firm but light pressure, burnish the surface until the finish is smooth, bright and glossy. Finish with long straight strokes.

TIP	CAUTION

Be sparing when using methylated spirits as too much will take off the surface you have just applied.

Repairing wood veneer

A wood veneer, by its very nature, enhances the surface of a cheaper material. But it is prone to chipping, blistering and loose edges. With a craft knife, adhesive and a strip of new veneer, such damage is straightforward to repair.

△ *This mahogany box, as the photograph above shows, was chipped and the veneer loose in places, yet it was possible to restore it to its former glory.*

Veneers have been used for centuries to give cheap surfaces a more expensive and attractive appearance. Wood veneers are usually hardwoods such as mahogany, teak, oak and walnut. Veneer is more prone to damage than solid pieces of wood because it is thin and glued to another surface. Old or badly glued veneer often becomes loose and must be glued back in place before further damage

occurs. Chipped veneer can be mended by cutting a replacement piece and glueing it in place.

It is not difficult to mend chipped veneer, but if the piece of furniture is particularly valuable it is better to have it professionally restored.

Blistered veneer

Blisters form under the veneer where the glue fails to stick. An old piece of furniture is likely to be stuck with animal glue, which may only need to be heated to be re-stuck. Modern pieces will need to have fresh glue applied and PVA adhesive is suitable. For using PVA, see pages 87-89.

Heating the glue
You will need
◇ Cardboard
◇ Domestic iron
◇ Clamp or weight

1 Lay a piece of thick cardboard over the blister. Move a hot iron slowly back and forward over the cardboard, to heat the glue beneath the veneer. Leave the cardboard in place and clamp or weight the blister for 24 hours. If the blister has not gone, proceed to the next method.

Re-gluing a blister
You will need
◇ Scalpel or craft knife
◇ Artists' brush
◇ PVA adhesive
◇ Cocktail stick
◇ Clamp or weight

1 Following the grain line, slit blister down the middle. Using an artists' brush, remove as much old glue and dirt as possible from under the blister.

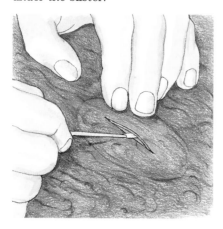

2 Hold down one side of the blister to open the crack. Put adhesive into the blister using a cocktail stick. Hold the glued side down and do the same on the other. Remove excess glue with a damp cloth. Clamp or weight the blister for 24 hours.

Loose veneer
If the edge of the veneer has started to come away, simply glue it back down. With care, hold the veneer away from the base and clean away as much old glue as possible. Apply the glue either with the nozzle of the adhesive container or a cocktail stick.

Replacing veneer
The new piece of veneer must match the surrounding grain as closely as possible and butt up exactly to the surrounding edges.

When buying veneer it is more important to match the pattern of the grain than the colour, as wood stains can be used to correct the colour. Many DIY shops and hardware stores sell veneer, or mail order suppliers can be found in woodwork and craft magazines.

Modern veneers are often too thin for the job, if so stick together a number of layers. Sand down the back of new veneer if it is too thick.

Mending chipped edges
You will need
◇ Tracing paper and pencil
◇ Masking tape and card
◇ Matching veneer
◇ Heavy duty craft knife
◇ PVC adhesive
◇ Clamp or weight

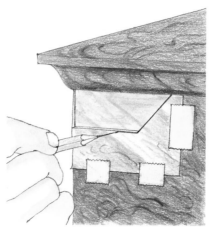

1 Cut away any jagged edges on the remaining veneer using a craft knife. Scrape off any old glue from the base. Tape tracing paper over the damaged area and draw around the outline.

2 Turn tracing paper over and place on back of replacement veneer. Trace outline on to veneer. Cut out using the craft knife. Glue in place. Clamp or weight the piece for 24 hours.

Replacing damaged areas
If the veneer is damaged in the body of the furniture, the procedure is similar to that given above. The replacement piece will be slightly bigger than the damaged area. The shape depends on the grain of the wood. If the wood has a straight line grain like larch, make a four sided shape slightly bigger than the damaged area. With a knotty grain such as walnut, make an irregular shape which will blend in more effectively. These shapes must be cut exactly to ensure a perfect fit.

1 Draw the shape on to a piece of tracing paper and transfer this to the new veneer as before. Cut out the replacement piece. Place this over the damaged area and, using the craft knife, draw around it leaving a scratched outline of the shape. Take away the veneer template and cut around the shape on the furniture.

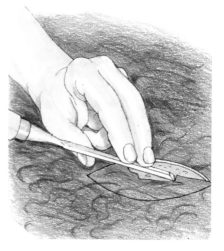

2 Gently remove any veneer within the shape by prising it away with a small chisel. Glue the new piece in place. Wipe off excess glue and clamp until dry.

TIP | CLAMPING

◆ Always put a block of wood or piece of card between the clamp or weight and the piece of wood.

◆ 'G' cramps can be used either directly over a glued spot, or in pairs to hold down a length of wood over the appropriate spot.

Renovating picture frames

*Beautifully framed pictures add atmosphere to a
room and the choice of frame and picture says as much about the
owner's personality as any other ornaments. Avoid the
expense of buying new picture frames by renovating existing
or secondhand frames.*

Frames

Whether you are looking for simple classic lines or intricately carved details, it is still possible to pick up a wide range of secondhand frames quite cheaply and renovate them to use with the existing picture or one of your own.

Some frames may be badly damaged and need a great deal of care and attention, although the majority only need cleaning and the minimum amount of repair. Whatever the repair remember that part of the charm of an old frame lies in the patina of age, so don't over-restore an interesting frame bought in a junkshop or market.

Wooden frames

The majority of frames are made of wood and those that have no special finish (simply waxed or varnished) are often instantly transformed when rubbed down with a wax or varnish remover. Dry bare wood can be revived by rubbing linseed oil into it — this enhances the grain and deepens the colour.

French polish To revive French polish rub on a mixture of ⅓ linseed oil, ⅓ vinegar and ⅓ methylated spirit. If you wish to remove the polish, wipe down with methylated spirit.

Lacquer If the frame has a high gloss lacquered finish you can disguise small scratches or marks with a little shellac mixed with a matching powder pigment (available from most art suppliers).

Paint Clean painted frames with a little soap and water, making sure that no water reaches the joints.

Veneer Should you have a frame that has been covered with a thin layer of fancy wood, the only sure way to remove a finish without damaging the veneer is to sand it off gradually by hand.

When purchasing frames always check for woodworm. If there are any tell-tale holes the frame will need treating with a proprietary solution. Don't worry if the joints are loose as these can easily be strengthened (see opposite).

Plaster moulded frames

Most plaster frames are moulded on a wooden base and, provided the plaster is not flaking or crumbling, repairing chipped areas is fairly straightforward.

Small areas can be built up with a filler. The repair is then retouched so that it matches the rest of the frame. For larger, more complicated areas you will need to take a mould from an undamaged section of this frame, make a cast and then glue the newly made section in place.

Should you have a plaster frame that seems beyond repair, don't throw it away; the moulding can often be chiselled away to expose a simple but serviceable wooden frame. To soften the plaster, cover it with damp rags for several days. Once the plaster has been removed, clean the wood by sanding down with glasspaper — if the wood be of poor quality, cover it with fabric.

Gilt frames

Gilt or gilded frames are mainly plaster frames finished with gold leaf or paint — wooden frames may be trimmed with a gilt. Before attempting any repair it is important to establish which finish has been used — if you are in any doubt ask a professional. Any repairs and cleaning must be carried out before applying the finish.

Gold leaf Antique frames are often gilded with real gold leaf. This is extremely thin and needs cautious treatment. If the frame is of value then you should leave any repair to a professional. Should the frame simply need cleaning, gently rub over it with a soft cloth or cotton wool and a mild solution of vinegar and water and buff up.

Gold paint This does not have the same lustre as gold leaf and is far easier to repair. The best finish is achieved with a wax-based paste (or wax gilt). It can be applied to the frame using a cloth or small brush. As the paint is wax-based it will not dry completely and needs to be buffed with a soft cloth, before a protective coat of varnish can be applied.

Metal frames

Small scratches can be concealed with a little metallic paint (available from art shops). Dirt can be removed by washing down with soap and water.

Wood veneer finish

Painted metal frame

Antique finish

Metal frame

Gold leaf finish

Wooden frame

Wood with paint effect finish

Painted wooden frame

Moulded gilt frame

Glossary of materials
Fillers
These are used to re-build missing areas on a frame.

Plaster frames — including those that are gilded — can be filled using fine grade Polyfilla, plastic wood filler (both are available from hardware stores) or plaster of Paris (from modelling shops). Alternatively use car body filler, (from car accessory shops).

Wooden frames Small chips can be filled with tinted wood filler (from hardware stores).

Large areas need to be replaced with new wood.

Shellac
A yellowish resin secreted from the lac insect which has been dissolved in alcohol to produce an almost instant-drying clear varnish. When tinted with dry powder pigment it is ideal for retouching lacquer.

Gesso
This is a fine plaster bound with glue size. Thin coats are applied to the frame to produce a smooth, hard, non-absorbent surface on which fine finishes, such as gilding, can be applied. Gesso is available from artist's suppliers.

Gold wax
This is a wax-based paste which is sold in tubes or pots in most art and craft shops. It is used to re-touch gold painted frames and is available in a number of shades — always choose a shade slightly darker than that of your frame. Gold wax sticks are also available. Specially formulated varnish that protects the wax is available from the same outlets.

Repairing wooden joints
The glue in a frame's joints tends to perish with age. Often a little additional glue or a nail is all that is needed. However in more serious cases the frame will need to be taken apart before the joints can be re-glued.

Applying additional glue
Pull the loose corner a little way apart and squeeze PVA woodworking adhesive into it, working it into the joint with a thin blade. Close the corner and hold in place until the glue adheres (at least 30 minutes). Special frame clamps are available from large hardware stores. Wipe away any excess glue with a damp cloth before it sets.

Dismantling joints

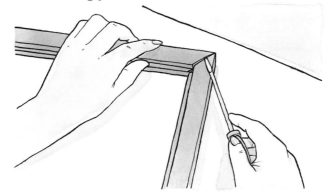

1 Working from the back of the frame, prise the corner joints apart with an old screwdriver or chisel. Number each section — when reassembling them you will find that no two mitres are the same.

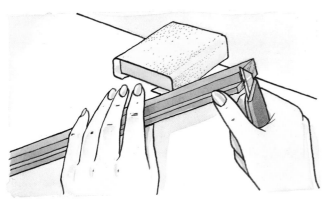

2 Dampen the old adhesive with water and scrape it away from the surface with a craft knife. Remove stubborn areas with glasspaper.

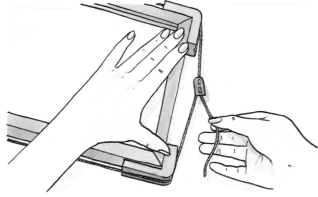

3 Apply a thin layer of PVA adhesive to the edges and press together. Add new nails if required and hold in place with a clamp.

Reinforcing joints
To reinforce the corners of large wooden frames cut small triangles from thin plywood — about ⅛in (3mm) thick — and glue and panel pin to the back of each corner.

Alternatively screw small metal plates (available from hardware stores) to each corner.

TIP	ADDING AGE

To give an aged look to a frame freshly treated with wax gilt:
◇ Streak a second darker shade of gold paint over the first prior to varnishing. Allow the lighter shade to show through on the high spots.
◇ Rub a little brown shoe polish over the frame and then buff off the excess on the high points.

Mending a moulded gilt frame

Old moulded gilt frames are easily damaged, but you can restore them with a little time and effort.

You will need
◇ Filler (see glossary)
◇ Wood glue
◇ Gold wax
◇ Palette knife
◇ Emery board
◇ Soft cloth
◇ Fine artist's brush
◇ Wax polish or varnish

△ *A dusty and damaged frame (above) is easy to restore (right).*

1 Mix together a small quantity of wood glue and filler — one part glue to three parts filler should give the right consistency. When you have a workable consistency, use a palette knife or your finger to pack the mixture into the chip.

2 Model the filler into roughly the correct shape. Leave to dry. Once dry, use an emery board to file away the excess filler so that it matches the original contours of the moulding as closely as possible.

3 Apply gold wax with a brush or soft cloth and leave to dry according to the manufacturer's instructions. Buff to a shine with a soft cloth.

To protect the paint and prevent tarnishing, coat with a thin layer of clear varnish or rub the frame with wax.

Repairing canvaswork

*Canvaswork will last for generations if it is
well cared for and any damage is mended as soon as possible.
Adding a backing fabric will support old canvaswork,
while holes and tears can be invisibly mended with a careful
choice of yarns and nimble stitching.*

The term canvaswork describes an item worked in counted thread stitch on a firm, open weave fabric. It is commonly used to upholster stools and chair seats, and also to make wall hangings or framed as pictures. The methods used to clean and repair the canvaswork will vary slightly depending on its end use, yet there are problems common to most items. These in-

◁ *This Georgian walnut wing chair illustrates how canvaswork becomes worn with use. Something as valuable as this chair, however, should be professionally restored.*

clude rust damage — from the nails holding the piece of canvas to the furniture or frame — holes, tears and loose threads.

The instructions here explain how to repair framed canvaswork or, alternatively, a piece of canvaswork that has been mounted on a stool or seat using tacks. Do not attempt to repair a chair that has been completely upholstered in canvaswork, or an item that is valuable. However, these instructions could be adapted to mend items such as loose covers.

Upholstered canvaswork

Canvaswork on furniture should be protected from the rigours of day-to-day wear and tear as much as possible. Always keep pets with sharp claws and teeth away from upholstery. When it is not on show, use loose covers to protect upholstery from dust, dirt and direct light. These can quickly be removed for special occasions.

Cleaning upholstery

Remove dust with the upholstery attachment of a vacuum cleaner. A special, nylon gauze can be pinned over the needlework to stop any rubbing against the threads.

The canvas must be taken off the furniture for cleaning and mending. Before washing a piece, make sure the canvaswork is colourfast or it will be ruined. Make up a cold solution of detergent. Place an absorbent pad behind an area of canvaswork and, using a white cloth, press the solution through the fabric. If colour runs, stop.

Backing the canvas

Some knowledge of upholstery is needed to remove and replace the canvaswork. Either learn how to do this (evening classes in upholstery are widely available) or ask an expert for advice.

The canvas is normally held in place with nails, which can often rust and damage the canvaswork. It is important to remove the nails before the rust has time to spread. This can be done two ways: by gently levering up the nails; or, if the canvas is badly rotted, by loosening the fibres around the nails first, removing the canvas, then prising out the old nails.

Put a backing on the canvaswork to support it and enable repair work to be done. A piece of open weave linen, about 2in (5cm) bigger

all round than the canvas, is suitable for the backing. The backing must be stretched taut so that it, not the canvaswork, takes the strain when someone sits on the seat. Wash the canvaswork *before* attaching it to the backing.

You will need
◇ Piece of open weave linen 2in (5cm) bigger all round than the canvas
◇ Tapestry frame
◇ Buttonhole thread and needle

1 Thoroughly wash the piece of linen to remove any dressing. Straighten the warp and weft while damp. Mount it in a tapestry frame and stretch it tightly.

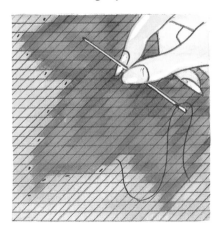

2 Lay the cleaned canvaswork on top of the linen. Pin in place. Stitch the two together. Use small stab stitch, working around patterned areas of the design, so that the stitches will not be seen. To hold the canvas firmly in place, stitch around as much of the pattern as possible; do not leave larger areas — more than 3in (7.5cm) square — unstitched.

3 Take the backing off the frame. The canvas will bubble up. Turn up the edges of backing twice to enclose canvas edge, covering the

old nail holes. Attach the canvas to the chair and cover the edges of the backing with a braid trim.

Mending a hole

Holes can be mended by putting a piece of canvas, with the same thread count as the original, between the canvas and the backing. The patch is then worked in threads of the same colour, using the pattern on a matching chair or similar area on the canvas as a guide. Study colour ranges of threads from various manufacturers to find the best match.

You will need
◇ Piece of canvas
◇ Matching threads
◇ Needle

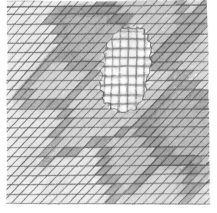

1 Attach the backing fabric as before but do not sew down the area around the hole. Position the canvas patch between the backing and the canvaswork, taking care to line up the warp and weft with the damaged canvas.

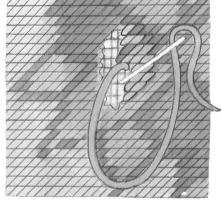

2 Work stitches according to the original pattern, taking needle through backing fabric. Work up to the sound stitches on original canvas. A gap of half a stitch may be left, but this will barely show once canvas has been remounted.

Mending a tear

Mend any tears in the canvas while it is being attached to the backing. Stitch over the torn area just once — if stitched too many times it will strain the canvas.

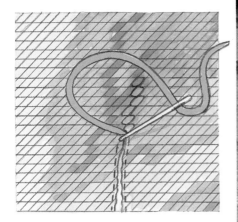

Stabilise the area around the tear by working stab stitch ¼in (6mm) from the torn edge. Using matching threads and repeating the original stitch used, work across the tear to cover the ragged edges.

Loose threads

Never cut off loose or unwanted threads. Use a latchet hook to pull the thread right through the canvas and backing fabric.

Framed canvaswork

Framed canvaswork can suffer similar problems to upholstered canvaswork — it can become dirty, despite being protected by glass; insects may get into the frame, eating the canvas and causing holes; a previous restorer may have used glue, which will damage the canvas; or it may need to be removed from the stretcher and re-stretched over acid free board.

General care

Take the canvas out of the frame. Carefully clean the glass inside and out. Using a nozzle attachment, vacuum the back of the canvaswork to remove any dust and insects. As with upholstery, nails often hold the canvaswork to the wooden stretcher. If these are rusty, remove

them as before. The canvas can be put on to a backing, as described earlier, but in this case it will not need to be pulled quite so taut.

Washing

Test all the colours in a canvas picture before attempting to wash it. Most pictures from the Victorian era have at least one colour that runs. Even when washed, the canvaswork picture is unlikely to come up sparkling clean.

Removing glue

If a canvaswork picture has been previously restored, it is possible that glue was used to hold the stitching, or the canvas, in place.

Determine what type of glue was used. Then test the canvas for colourfastness, as it will have to be

△ *A close-up section of the Georgian chair (opening page) reveals worn areas.*

washed. Spirit based glues will need to be treated with a solvent, so first test an inconspicuous area of the canvas for an adverse reaction to the solvent.

Flour paste is very damaging as it attracts insects, which then eat into the canvas. To remove flour paste, the canvas will have to be soaked for 24 hours, so more vigorous testing must be followed. Press threads from the canvaswork between two white cloths that have been soaked in a washing solution of a non-ionic, low-foam liquid detergent. Place them in a polythene bag for 24 hours. If dyes do not run, proceed.

To remove flour paste
You will need
◇ Thoroughly cleaned and rinsed container
◇ Polythene film
◇ White cloth
◇ De-ionised water
◇ Plastic spatula

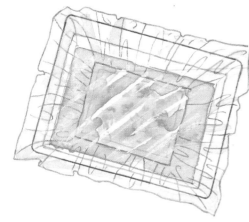

1 Put the sampler — glue side up — in a suitably sized container lined with polythene film. Cover the canvas in de-ionised water and leave to soak for 24 hours. This will make glue soften and swell.

▽ *Beautiful canvaswork upholstery needs to be protected from day-to-day wear and tear.*

2 Take hold of the polythene film and lift the canvas out of the water. Take it off the film and lie it on a piece of clean white cotton, glue side up. Gently remove the glue using a plastic spatula or your fingernail. When as much glue as possible has been removed, wash the canvas carefully. Do not wring the fabric as it causes damage.

Replacing the stretcher
If the stretcher needs replacing because of damage, lace the canvaswork over a piece of acid free board rather than nailing it into a wooden frame. If the canvas is quite wide, use two or three short pieces of thread — these can be tightened individually.

You will need
◇ Acid free board
◇ Scissors, needle and drawing pins
◇ Strong button thread

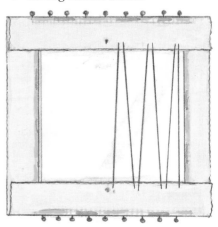

1 Cut a piece of acid free board to the size of the frame. Lay out the canvas, backing side up, and smooth it out. Centre the board on top of the canvas backing. Fold top and lower edges over board and gently pull taut.

2 Pin the folded edges to board. Stitching through both the canvas and backing, take the thread from one folded edge to the other in a zigzag motion. Pull the thread firm as you work, then fasten off securely.

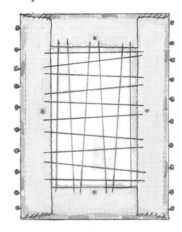

3 Take out the pins. Fold the side edges over the back and pin in place. Lace as above. Stitch down corners. Remove pins.

Re-caning chair seats

The attractive canework used to create woven chair
panels is extremely hardwearing, but it can deteriorate badly with time.
There is little you can do to repair a
split and broken seat, but you can re-cane the panels to
make delapidated furniture as good as new.

Traditional caning

Cane furniture has been popular for over 300 years, and many traditionally worked chairs still survive today. Old canework is often expensive, however, attractive antiques can still be purchased relatively cheaply if the cane seat has sagged and broken.

Restoring such chairs to their former light and delicate style is immensely satisfying, and creating the intricate-looking patterns is just a matter of technique and patience. Check that the piece you intend to re-cane was traditionally worked with the cane anchored in holes. Some modern pieces use sheets of cane, stapled in place.

What is cane?

The material used to cane furniture is harvested from a creeper grown in South East Asia. It has a tough outer bark which, when peeled away, reveals an inner core coated in a tough, shiny layer. This layer is stripped from the core and cut into standard widths; it is this which is used for furniture caning.

The widths of cane are numbered from 1-6. No 1 is the smallest, measuring 1.7mm, and No 6 is the largest at 3.5mm. When buying cane to renovate a chair, try to select the same size of cane as was used for the original seat. As a general rule, the smaller and closer the holes of your seat, the smaller size cane you will need to use. The most commonly used sizes are No 4 for the seat, No 6 for the beading that finishes the edge of the seat and No 2 for the couching that stitches it down. Cane is available from all good craft shops, or from specialist suppliers by mail order. It is also available ready-woven.

Specialist equipment

You don't need a lot of equipment for caning; most of the things you need can be found in the home.
A craft knife for cutting cane the scissors cannot reach and for making sharp points on the pegs.
A clearing tool for cleaning the holes. You can cut the end off an old screwdriver or use a large nail; the diameter should not be more than $\frac{1}{8}$in (3mm) on a chair where the holes are $\frac{1}{4}$in (6mm) in diameter.
Plastic golf tees or wooden dowelling are essential for jamming the cane into the holes and holding the cane taut while weaving. Use dowelling, slightly larger than the holes, shaved to a point.
A bodkin, shell bodkin or curved cane threader is useful to help weave the cane in and out if your fingers aren't very nimble.

Caning a seat base

The method of caning a seat base is quite straightforward. Most seats are woven in the traditional 'six-way' pattern (also known as seven-step). This pattern is made up of two vertical 'settings', two horizontal 'weavings' and two diagonal 'crossings'. Other patterns are sometimes used for caned furniture which are worked in a similar way (see page 74). If you work methodically, keeping the page open at the step you are working, you should have success every time.

You will need
◇ Sharp scissors and a craft knife
◇ Clearing tool
◇ Hand drill to clear out stubborn holes
◇ Fine grade wire wool
◇ Cane in the correct sizes for the seat, the beading and the couching
◇ Centre cane for pegging
◇ Golf tees or wooden dowels
◇ Bodkin, shell bodkin or threader
◇ Bucket, old towel and hammer

Preparation

Gather all your tools and materials together and, if working indoors, place a few sheets of newspaper on the floor to protect the floor covering. Before you begin to cut away the old broken cane, inspect the chair thoroughly for any loose joints or broken sections that might need to be repaired. Check carefully for woodworm too, and treat with a proprietary liquid, then stop the holes if you find any evidence of past infestation.

You may also want to consider the eventual finish of your chair. If it is to be stripped, painted or varnished, or even given a thorough clean and polish, this must be done before the chair is re-caned.

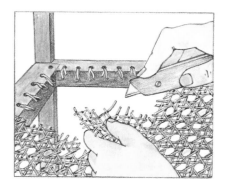

1 Cut away the old cane with the craft knife, keeping the panel intact so that you can refer to the pattern if necessary while you are working.

2 Remove the cane beading on the upper and underside of the rails, taking care not to damage the chair with the point of the knife.

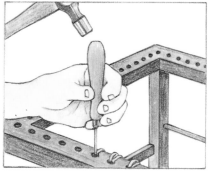

3 Push out any old pegs and remaining cane from the holes using the clearing tool. If any of the old pegs have wedged fast inside the holes, drill them out with a hand drill rather than risk damaging the frame by knocking them too hard with a hammer.

4 Clean the chair rail of any accumulated dust and dirt using fine grade wire wool and soapy water. Rinse well, and attend to any repairs before you start.

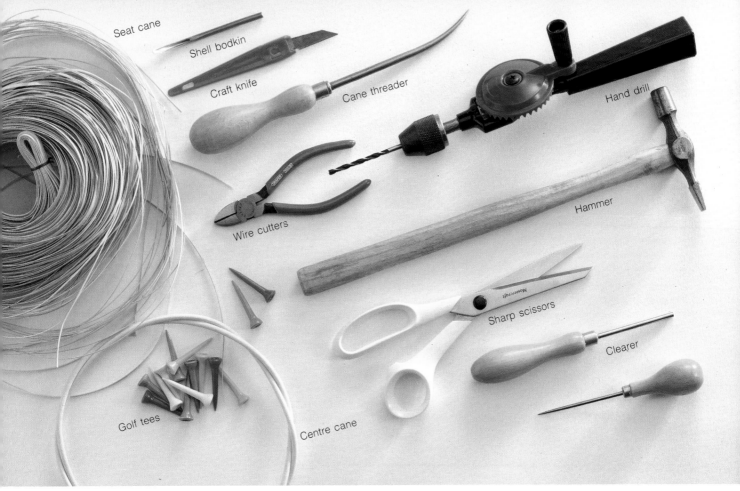

Seat cane

Shell bodkin

Craft knife

Cane threader

Hand drill

Wire cutters

Hammer

Sharp scissors

Clearer

Golf tees

Centre cane

How to cane

Pull a small quantity of cane from your bundle and soak for a few minutes in a bowl of warm water.

Cane, like satin fabric, has a smooth and a rough grain. Always try to work with the grain; it is easier on your fingers and prevents snagging.

1 Setting Take a workable length of seat cane and peg with a golf tee or wooden dowel into the centre hole on the back rail of the seat, making sure that the smooth, shiny surface of the cane is facing upwards.

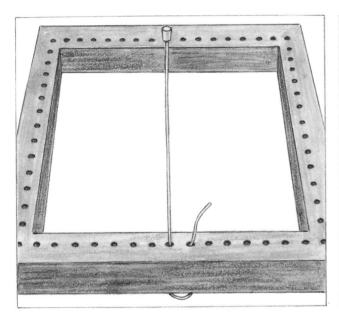

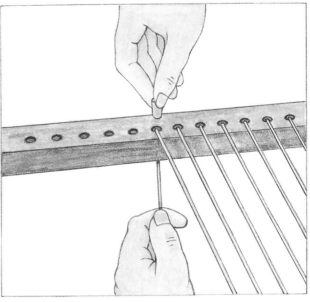

2 Pass the other end of the cane down through the opposite hole on the front rail, loop under and pass up through the next hole ready to begin the next vertical setting.

3 Continue until every hole is filled. When you come to the end of your length of cane, peg firmly with a dowel and begin a fresh length in the next hole. Pull the cane taut but avoid stretching it as some shrinkage will occur naturally as the material dries out. Leave the ends on the underside loose — these will be tied off once your weaving is complete.

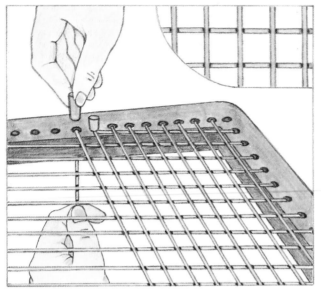

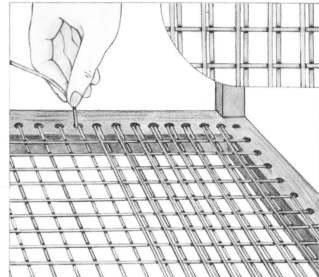

4 **Weaving** Begin the horizontal weaving in the same way as the setting, starting in the back hole of the side rail. Continue to the front until every hole is filled.

5 **Work the second setting** in the same way as the first, starting once again in the centre but this time at the front of the rail. Position the cane over the top of the previous two layers and slightly to the left of the first setting.

6 **For the second weaving,** worked from right to left, the cane is woven between the two settings but comes through the same holes and in the same direction as the first weaving. You do not need to pull the cane through every time. Work a few weavings and then pull it taut.

7 **Diagonals** Begin the first diagonals in the first hole at the back of the left-hand rail. Weave towards the hole diagonally opposite at the front of the right hand rail. Work with one hand on top and the other beneath the seat.

The cane must be woven under the settings and over the weavings in a 'step' fashion. Once you reach halfway you will need to work the cane into the corner holes. Take the cane through the hole and down under the rail, make a loop, and feed the cane back up through the same hole. Use a peg to hold it in place.

8 Check your work carefully at this stage; if the cane is not woven correctly, the edges will rub together and break.

9 To work the second diagonal, do the opposite to the weaving on the first diagonal. The corners are used twice in the diagonal caning.

Finishing a caned seat

*There are two methods of fastening the ends on
a caned seat — pegging and couching. Both provide an attractive
finish that prevents the handwoven panel from sagging.
If you consider hand-weaving and finishing too time-consuming,
why not try using ready-made sheet cane?*

*A newly caned chair
seat has been tidied
up around the edges
using a couched
finish.*

Pegged finish

△ *Traditionally, most seats were
pegged in every hole with wooden
dowels or sections of centre cane
to hold the panel in place.*

1 Cut lengths of centre cane
slightly shorter than the depth
of the chair rail. Check the fit. If
necessary, whittle the ends with a
craft knife to enable the pegs to
slide easily into the holes.

2 Starting in a corner, hammer a
peg into each of the holes until
the ends are nearly level with the
seat. Using a nail punch, bradawl or
old screwdriver knock the pegs
down just below the surface of the
seat. Take care not to knock the
surrounding wood or split the
edges of the cane.

3 The pegs should be wedged in
tight enough to retain the
tautness of the cane webbing. Don't
be tempted to glue the pegs in
place, as they will be almost
impossible to remove if you wish to
re-cane the seat at some point in
the future.

4 Finish the underside by
trimming away any odd lengths
of cane with scissors as close to the
bottom rail as possible.

Couched finish

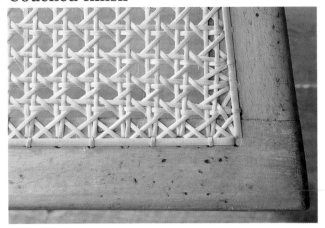

Although couching is slightly harder for the home renovator than pegging, once mastered it provides an extremely neat and attractive finish.

Couching makes an ideal finish for straight-sided seats, but can be more complicated to work on curved surfaces as it is sometimes tricky to keep the couched cane (also known as beading cane) in place so that it covers the pegs neatly.

With a couched finish, every alternate hole is pegged and a strip of wide cane (generally No 6) is laid over the holes and anchored to the chair with a strand of fine cane (generally No 2) woven through the empty holes. You will inevitably still be able to see the peg in the hole you start from, however, all the other pegs should be completely covered by the cane.

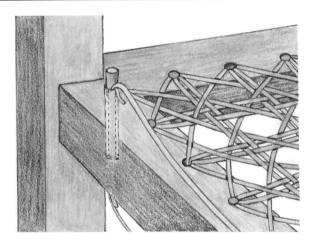

1 Cut four lengths of wide beading cane, each one slightly longer than the edge of the seat. With a golf tee or wooden dowel, peg the first length of No 6 cane and a strand of No 2 cane into the back left-hand corner hole, No 6 protruding from the top and No 2 protruding from the underside.

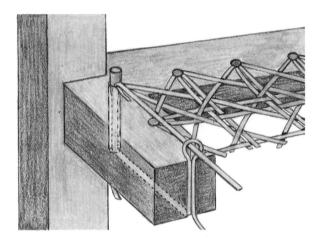

2 Bring a damp piece of thin No 2 cane up through the first unpegged hole, over the No 6 cane and back down through the same hole, to form a small loop that will hold the No 6 cane flat. Pull the cane taut and permanently peg in place from below.

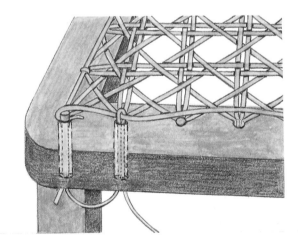

3 Continue the couching along the rail. When you reach the corner, thread the two canes for the next side of the chair frame through the corner hole and peg. Position the peg so that the next piece of beading cane will cover the peg when you fold it down to start the next line of couching. Complete the remaining two sides in the same manner.

TIP STAINING AND PAINTING CANE

New cane is naturally light in colour. With time it will darken slowly to a rich golden hue, but if your chair is made of a dark wood, you may want to stain the cane panel to match. You can achieve deeper tones using a non-water-based wood stain.

First, stain a left-over strand to establish whether the shade is right. Then, using a cloth, carefully rub the stain all over the caned panel.

If the chair has a paint finish, you may want to colour the cane to match. Choose a microporous paint, which has a slight flex to it and is designed to allow wood to breath. Once the cane is painted, it will still be able to move naturally without any risk of the paint flaking or cracking.

---

4 Once the beading is finished, replace the golf tee or temporary peg with a cane peg. Trim off the ends of the cane on the underside of the rail, dampening and tying in any remaining lengths.

Using sheet cane

Modern furniture is often caned with pre-woven sheets. These are glued rather than pegged in position. Although not as strong as traditional caning, it is useful for items such as radiators covers and screens.

Cane sheeting is available by the yard (metre) in widths of 24in (60cm). The sheets need to be soaked to make them pliable. For a neat finish, the edges can be covered with wooden beading, stained or painted to match the surrounding area.

You will need
◇ Cane sheeting
◇ Soft pencil
◇ Scissors
◇ Staple gun
◇ Craft knife
◇ Wood glue
◇ Panel pins
◇ Wooden beading
◇ Mitre box
◇ Hammer

▽ *The blond sheet cane flat headboard and sidetable insets are simple to fit secured with beading. The rocking chair is not so easy to re-cane. Sheet cane needs to be handled expertly to make it strong enough for seating.*

1 Mark out the area to be covered and measure up for the panel of cane, leaving a ½in (1cm) allowance all round.

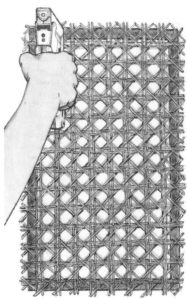

2 Soak the cane in a warm bath for about 10 minutes and then cut out the piece, taking care to follow the pattern correctly.

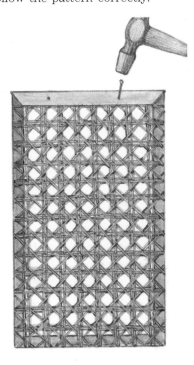

3 Using a staple gun, fix the cane in place, starting at the centre top of the panel. The staples should be positioned so that they will be covered by the beading. If you are applying the cane to the back of a space to be covered, the position of the staples won't matter.

4 Trim away the rough edges of the cane with a sharp craft knife, just inside the marked line. Measure and cut the beading accurately, mitring the corners. Glue and pin in place.

PATTERN LIBRARY

Traditional caners wove their patterns in a variety of attractive patterns. Of the four examples shown below, only the five-way standard and the double Victoria are really suitable for chair seats. The others are too weak to support regular use. The four-way standard and the single Victoria are quick, easy and ideally suited for caning other types of furniture such as radiator panels, cane screens and headboards.

You can work these patterns in a similar way to the traditional six-way pattern shown on pages 68-70. Simply follow the colour coded steps to achieve perfect results.

The four-way standard

This is a simple pattern, ideal for caned panels. Work the horizontals and verticals in the same way as the traditional six-way pattern, followed by the diagonals. Step 1, red; step 2, yellow; step 3, green; step 4, blue.

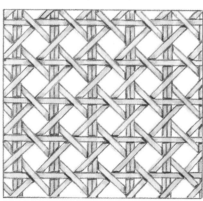
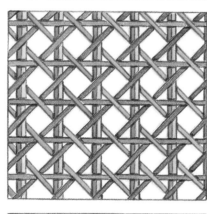

The five-way standard

Work in the same way as the four-way standard, but double the cane on the first step. Step 1, red; step 2, yellow; step 3, green; step 4, blue; step 5, orange.

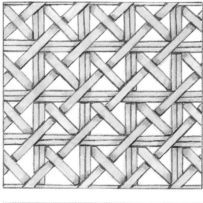
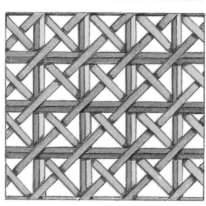

The double Victoria

Double the cane in steps 1 and 2, then work the first diagonal straight across the top. The second diagonal is worked in the same way as the single Victoria. Step 1, red; step 2, yellow; step 3, green; step 4, blue; step 5, mauve; step 6, orange.

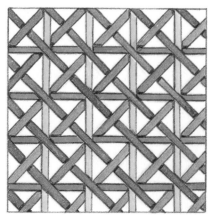

The single Victoria

Work the horizontals and verticals in the same way as the traditional six-way pattern, with the first diagonal lying straight across the top. The second diagonal is woven under the cross formed by steps 1 and 2, and over the first diagonal. Step 1, red; step 2, yellow; step 3, blue; step 4, green.

Rush seating 1

*Rushed seats tend to collapse over the years,
but they need not be discarded. Repair them using the technique
of rushing. Available in a range of colours
from dark green and orange to warm yellows and browns, this
natural fibre gives highly rewarding results.*

Rushing

Rush-seated chairs and stools have been made in Europe as far back as the Middle Ages. Today rushing is as popular as ever; its texture and colouring make it an ideal accompaniment to all styles of furniture and soft furnishings.

Rush seats and footstools are made by twisting together lengths of rush to form a coil. The coil is then wound around the seat frame in a continuous strand to form the seat — the thinner the coil and tighter the twist, the finer the finished seat will be. New rushes are twisted in as required and the way in which they are wound around the frame will determine the finished effect.

What is rush?

There are two main varieties of rush — or to give them their correct name, reeds — freshwater rush (known as green rush) and salt rush. Both varieties are grown all over Europe. Salt rush tends to be of better quality, however, freshwater rushes are more readily available. Rushes can be bought from specialist suppliers or direct from the grower.

Rushes are bought by the bolt. This is a large conical bundle about 6ft (1.8m) high and weighing about 4lb (2kg) — an average chair takes about two-thirds of a bolt. Bolts can be stored on end, though loose rushes should be kept level. Rushes should be stored in a dry, well-ventilated area.

Rushes are found in rivers, ponds and marshy areas. If you wish to pick your own, you should do so in late summer. Cut each piece as close to the ground as possible and dry flat. Do not tie them into bundles until completely dry, otherwise mould will form rendering the rushes useless.

If you have trouble purchasing rushes at certain times of the year, it is possible to achieve a similar effect using seagrass (coarse grass twisted into a rope), artificial rush (made from paper) or cord (known as whipcord).

Equipment

You do not need many specialist tools when rushing. There are some special tools, but you may be able to improvise with tools found around the home.

Rush needle This is for easing the last few coils into place and can be bought from craft suppliers. Alternatively, use a large carpet needle.

Padding stick This is used to stuff any gap between the layers of rushes. It can also be used to line up the lengths of rush by forcing them against the side of the chair legs. Use a thin, smooth wedge-shaped piece of wood — a kitchen spatula will do.

Craft knife A strong, sharp knife is needed to trim the rough ends of the rushes underneath the seat.

Scissors Large scissors can be used to trim the rushes before commencing work.

String Soft string is used to anchor the first set of rushes to the chair frame.

▽ *Rushes grow in and around water. Crops are normally harvested every alternate year as this allows the rushes to grow to full maturity.*

Dutch fresh water

Spanish

Seagrass

Portuguese

Dutch salt water

Coiled paper

Preparation

Even if only a small part of the rushed seat is damaged, it is still advisable to replace the entire covering. Before removing the damaged rushing it is a good idea to make notes and sketches of the damaged seat, you can then refer back to them when working the pattern.

Always carry out any renovation to the frame of the chair prior to rushing and apply any finishes.

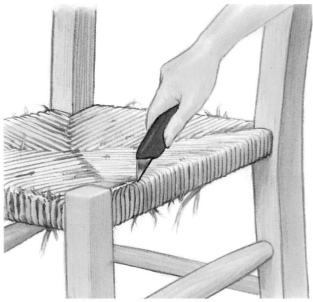

1 Many rush seats are finished with a strip of beading, positioned between the chair legs and around the rushing. This should be prised away with a chisel or claw hammer.

2 Remove the rushing by slicing it open along the rails with a craft knife, taking care not to cut into the wood. Keep the old seat intact as this can be used for reference.

3 Sand down the wooden rails underneath the rush. If the rails are at all rough they will cut and scrape the new rushes which will eventually weaken and damage the new seat.

Rushing a seat base

The basic rushing technique shown here is for any regular shaped seat (that is, square or oblong in shape). If you have a slightly shaped seat — one that is wider at the front than the back — you will need to refer to the alternative starting techniques which are shown on page 80.

Before you start, sort the rushes into large, medium and thin sizes — judge them from the thick end (the butt) rather than the tip.

The rushes must be dampened before use to make them supple. To dampen the rushes, place them in a bath of cold or tepid water for one to two minutes — place the butt ends in first then carefully fold around the thinner ends so the rushes are completely submerged in the water. Remove them and fold in half before tightly wrapping them in a towel. Only dampen as many rushes as you think you require and remove any dead or broken pieces.

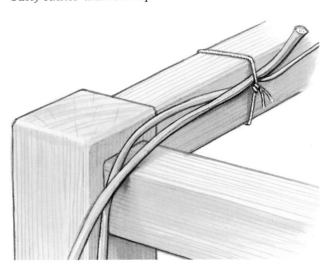

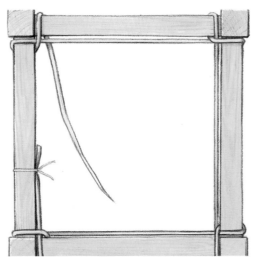

1 Pick out two lengths of rush. Their size will depend on how thick you want the coil to be (use the old seat as a guide). Hold them together — tip to butt — and tie one end to the left-hand side of the seat frame, so that the knot and rush ends are on the inside.

2 Twist the two rushes together to form a tight coil. Weave around the frame following the sequence above and keeping the coil taut. Continue twisting the rushes when working on the top of the seat and down the front of the rail — the rushes underneath should be kept flat.

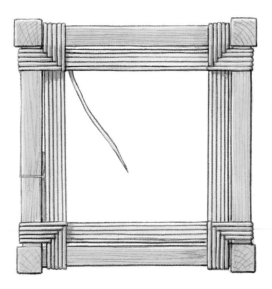

3 Continue weaving and twisting the rushes around the frame of the chair seat by repeating the sequence. Make sure that the two crossings that form the corners of the seat are always at right angles to each other.

4 To work in new lengths of rush, use a reef knot or half-hitch on the underside of the seat — avoid doing this near a corner as it may distort the weaving. Always keep the coil as even as possible by combining different sized rushes — for example, two rushes as before, three or four thin ones, or one thick one. When using one thick rush you will need to add a thin one with a half-hitch as the rush begins to thin.

5 When you have completed about a third of the seat you will see that a small gap has formed between the upper and lower layers of rush. Turn the seat over and, working from the underside, pack the gap with small, dry pieces of rush by folding them in into small bunches and pushing them deep into the pocket with a padding stick — do not use too much padding at a time, but build it up slowly. Leave the unfinished seat to dry for 24 hours.

◆ TIP   TWISTING AND TYING RUSHES

Twisting

Tying

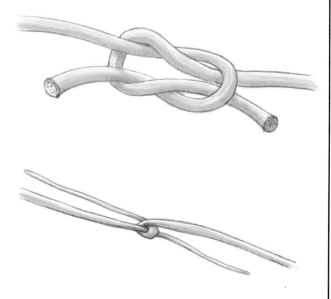

Do not twist one rush around another, but work both together as shown (right). To expel trapped air, grip the rushes between your finger and thumb and give a sharp tug, running your fingers down the length. You will hear a slight popping sound as the air is released.

As the end of a length of rushes is reached, you will need to join a new length to it. The neatest way to do this is to knot them together underneath the seat with a reef knot (top) or half-hitch (below).

Rush seating 2

*Once you have started on a rushing project,
finishing the rushwork is a fairly straightforward and
satisfying task. Should you have a chair seat
that is not a regular shape but tapered, then a different
starting technique is necessary.*

△ *Simple Spanish-style ladderback
chairs have been rushed to
complement this traditionally rustic
dining area. The mellow tones of
the seats echo the warm earthy
colours of the wood and stone.*

▷ *A thin wooden trim around the
outer edge of the seat (known as
beading) not only provides a neat
and attractive finish, but also helps
to protect the rushwork from wear
and tear.*

Finishing the seat

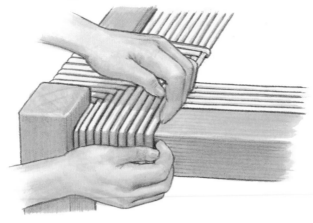

1 When the rush has dried out for 24 hours, press the dried rushes together by forcing them against the chair legs with your fingers or a padding stick. Continue weaving the rushes as before, padding out every few inches.

2 As you reach the centre you will have difficulty in padding the seat. Bridge the padding across the gap and weave over and under it. You may also find there is no room to knot in new rushes. Instead tuck the butt end of the new rush into the centre of the seat and twist old and new rushes together.

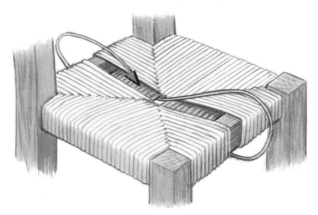

3 Unless the seat is square, you will fill one set of opposite rails before the other. Mark the centre of the rails, then fill the gap by weaving in a figure of eight. You will need to use a rush needle to weave in the final few coils — pack in as many as possible as the rushes will shrink when dry.

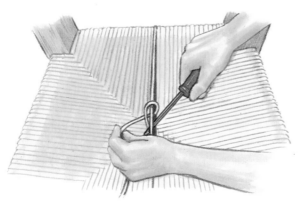

4 To tie off the final end, wrap it over the back rail and bring it through the centre of the seat to the underside. Lift up a central coil (use an old

Shaped seats

On many seats, the front rail is wider than the back, so that the side rails are angled to form a slightly tapered shape. You have to use a different starting technique to fill in the 'wedge' at each end of the front rail.

1 Tie the first rush coil to the left-hand side of the seat frame in the usual way. Wrap the coil over the front bar, around the side bar and across to the other side, then around the opposite side bar and front bar, keeping the rush taut at all times. Cut off the coil to match the left-hand side and tie it to the right-hand rail.

2 Repeat this process, building up five or six coils of rush, until the length of the front rail, which remains exposed, matches the width of the back rail.

As an alternative, build up the front rail by wrapping the coil twice around the front rail on every other row until the space left along the front and back rails is equal.

screwdriver for this) and hook the last coil through it. Pull through and knot firmly. Trim the seat of any free ends. If the seat was finished with a wood trim, replace it, knocking the tacks in gently with a fine tack hammer.

Repairing old chairs

*Battered wooden chairs are a common sight
in second hand shops. Basic problems such as loose joints
and damaged seats are straightforward to mend
and, with a bit of imagination, chairs can be turned into
individually styled pieces of furniture.*

Neglected old wooden chairs can be bought very cheaply in second hand shops. Yet many have interesting features which have been overlooked and, despite their hopeless appearance, most need only a few repairs like re-gluing joints or replacing rails to make them sound again. Once repaired, each chair can be given an individual look with a decorative seat cover or a paint or varnish finish to complement its features. To bring out the character of each chair, paint fine carved details in a colour that contrasts with the rest of the chair. A number of different chairs can be made to look like a set if they are decorated in the same way.

Re-gluing loose joints

Loose joints need to be taken apart and then glued firmly back in place. Make the old glue as soft as possible before attempting to dismantle the joint. Use a mallet only when necessary and only on the sturdiest parts of the joint.

Make sure all traces of old glue are removed from the joint before applying the new glue; some glues react badly with others and the bond will be stronger if the glue is holding wood to wood rather than wood to old glue.

Resin-based glues give a very strong bond and should be used where a very strong joint is needed, for example in the chair back. PVA is a good, easy-to-use alternative. Professional restorers prefer animal glue which is soluble in water, but this is fiddly to prepare.

You will need

◇ Warm, damp cloth
◇ Pliers (optional)
◇ Mallet with carpet covering the head
◇ Wood glue
◇ Sash cramp and wooden blocks or webbing and panel pins

1 Wring out a cloth in very hot water and wrap it around the joint to warm and loosen the glue.

2 Gently prise the joint apart using a twisting pulling motion. Use pliers to grip smaller pieces like dowel bars. If necessary, loosen the joint by knocking around it with a carpet-covered mallet.

3 When the pieces have been separated, clean off all traces of glue. Apply new glue and fit the joint together. A few taps with the covered mallet may be needed to drive the pieces home. Wipe off any excess glue while it is still wet using a damp cloth or sponge — it is impossible to remove the glue once it has dried.

Clamping

Clamp the joint firmly while the glue dries. Use a level surface to prevent the joint setting with a twist. The method of clamping used depends on the position of the joint. The glued area should be left to dry for 24 hours.

TIP	FINISHES

◇ Always use glues and paints in a well ventilated area to avoid a build up of fumes.

◇ Clean away any sawdust and dirt from the chair and surrounding area before starting to paint or varnish.

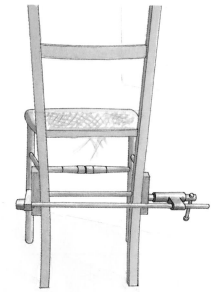

For two straight surfaces, for example when your clamping the stretchers to the legs, use a bar or sash cramp. Put blocks of wood between the cramp and the chair to prevent the cramp from damaging the chair surface.

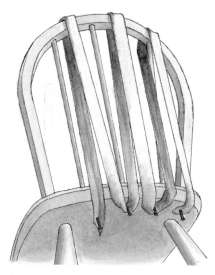

On a curved chair back use rope or rubber webbing (better because it is less likely to slip). Hammer panel pins into the underside of the seat at 3in (7.5cm) intervals, attaching the end of the webbing to the seat with the first pin. Wrap webbing over top of chair then bring it down, around a pin. Continue like this along the width of the back, pulling the webbing taut. When glue is dry, remove webbing and pins.

◁ *A missing bolt holding the leg to the seat and a split in the support bar were the only structural faults with this chair. The wood had lost most of its varnish leaving it unprotected and scruffy.*

▽ ▷ *The unusual reptile scale-like patterning of the wood was an obvious feature to highlight. To do this the surface was built up using latex paints. Red was applied as the base colour. Two shades of green were then applied very sparingly, one after the other. This made the most of the wonderful wood texture and used an unusual blend of colours.*

Re-dowelling

Replacing stretchers (the horizontal bars running between the legs) and spindles (the vertical bars on the back of chairs) is a common repair job. If the bar is straight, replace it with a length of dowelling from a hardware store. Take the old piece with you to ensure that you get the right diameter dowelling. More intricate pieces may be taken from a matching chair which is beyond repair. Or have a copy made by a wood turner. Keep the old piece so the turner can work from it.

Remove the damaged stretcher or spindle by the method described right. Note whether the end of the bar is tapered as it enters the joint — the replacement piece will have to be shaped the same way.

You will need

In addition to the tools and materials already listed under re-gluing old joints:
◇ Length of dowel
◇ Saw
◇ Drill
◇ File

1 Saw off the broken pieces of dowel as close to the joint as possible. Note whether the piece within the joint is smaller than the piece cut away, indicating that it is tapered at the end.

2 Drill out the piece left in the joint using a drill bit which matches the diameter of the hole. Drill straight into the hole or the replacement piece of dowel will not go in properly.

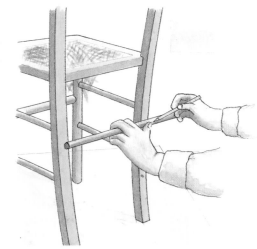

3 Mark the replacement dowel at length required, remembering to include the amount which will be hidden in the joint. If necessary taper ends using a file. Glue and clamp as described before.

Mending split wood

Round chairs often have bent wood which has been steamed into shape incorporated in the back or between the legs. This often splits as the wood dries out with age but is easily glued back in place.

The type of clamp used will vary depending on the position of the split, but usually a 'G' cramp will do the job.

1 Heat a cloth by dipping it in hot water. Wring it out, leaving the cloth quite damp. Wrap cloth around the split wood and leave for 15 minutes to soften it.

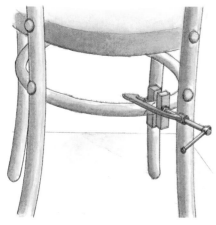

2 Remove cloth. The wood will be supple and will easily be persuaded back into shape. Apply glue, wipe away excess and clamp using a 'G' cramp. Protect the wood by putting wooden blocks between the cramp and the chair.

Decorative effects

Once the basic frame has been made sound, decide how to decorate the chair. Look at the chair carefully to see whether it has any interesting features which could be highlighted. For example, decorative carving can be emphasized with paint while an unusual wood texture may lend itself to a special paint effect such as oiling or waxing, which brings out the grain. (For details on how to varnish, oil and wax wood, turn to pages 47-52.)

If the seat is damaged it will have to be replaced, offering another creative opportunity. You may want to replace the seat anyway to give the chair a more interesting look. Use ¼in (6mm) plywood or medium density fibreboard (MDF) for the seat. Do not use hardboard because it flexes too much.

△ *Here, the cane has been replaced with a plywood seat, held in place with decorative brass tacks. A groove, picked out in paint, adds a touch of detail The wood has been waxed to bring out the natural warm, honey colour.*

Upholstering a seat

An upholstered pad is ideal for replacing a broken cane seat, though the technique can be used on any seat. Before re-upholstering the seat, strip away the cane and paint or stain the chair, depending on the finish desired. It will then be easier to choose a fabric which coordinates with the finish.

You will need
◇ Plywood or MDF
◇ Marker and ruler
◇ Saw
◇ Sandpaper
◇ 2-3in (5-7.5cm) thick foam padding
◇ Utility knife
◇ Calico or sturdy cotton twill
◇ Sturdy top fabric
◇ Staple gun and staples or tacks
◇ Drill
◇ Screws
◇ Felt tip pen

1 Place seat of the chair upside down on the plywood, making sure that the plywood is against the back of the chair. Draw around the inside opening of the seat.

2 Remove the seat. Using a ruler, mark a border ¾-1in (2-2.5cm) around the shape, depending on the chair frame: do not make the border too narrow or it will not cover the old cane holes; too large and the frame of the chair will not make a nice border around the shape.

▷ *A cane chair, similar to the one pictured far left, was sponge painted, then given an upholstered seat. A thin cord round the seat neatly covers the join.*

△ *The fabric established the colour for the chair. The frame was painted yellow and left to dry. It was then sponged in peach, followed by green, and finally a lighter yellow to give this lovely delicate mottled effect. Details were picked out in green.*

3 Cut out the seat shape along outer edge of border and sand the edges. Place the plywood seat on the foam padding and draw around it with a felt tip pen. Cut out foam with a utility knife.

4 Place padding in position on plywood. Cut out piece of cotton large enough to wrap over pad and overlap plywood base by 1in (2.5cm). Smooth over the seat and secure with ¼in (6mm) staples or tacks on the underside. Cut out top fabric 1in (2.5cm) larger all round than cotton. Put in place, smoothing out any wrinkles and neatly folding over corners. Tuck under raw edge. Fasten as before.

5 Drill pilot holes in the chair seat frame ½in (1.2cm) in from the inner edge of border at each corner and in the middle of each side. Position seat and screw firmly in place from the underside.

Drill-hole patterned chair seat

Another simple but effective seat is a pattern of drilled holes. Either drill into the original seat or cut a replacement piece of plywood and fix it to the chair seat. Make sure the drill bits are sharp and work slowly to prevent very frayed edges, which take a lot of sanding. Take the pattern from an old chair or make up your own.

1 Work out a pattern and transfer it to tracing paper. Put the traced design in position on the seat and hold in place with masking tape. Using a small nail, prick through the paper hard enough to leave indentations, marking the seat where each hole should be. Remove tracing paper.

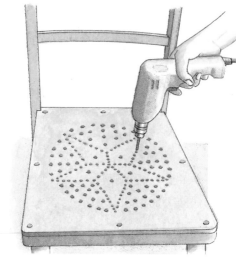

2 Slowly drill the holes. If more than one size of hole is required, drill all the holes needed in one size before changing the drill bit to another size.

▽ *Despite having no seat, the soft curves and carved detail of this chair immediately suggest it has the potential to be eye-catching.*

▷ *The surface was painted in a shocking blue base which was then lightly worked over in a lighter shade of blue and white paint. The paint was then sanded back to the wood in places. A final rub down with fine wire wool brought a sheen to the surface.*

▽ *A new seat was cut out of plywood and patterned with drill holes before the frame was painted.*

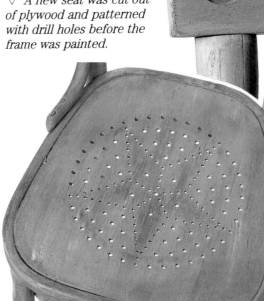

Choosing and applying adhesives

The wide range of adhesives available can make choosing the right one for the job a daunting experience. Here we clarify what is available in the shops, how to select the right product and how to apply the adhesives to ensure perfect results.

There are adhesives available today for sticking almost every type of material to any type of surface, but it can be confusing trying to select the right one for the job.

The adhesive you choose for any job will usually depend on the items to be stuck together. There is a 'right' adhesive for most jobs. That is, one that has been especially formulated for the type of materials it will be applied to and therefore gives maximum performance.

By following manufacturers' instructions carefully and choosing the right type of adhesive, it is possible to ensure a perfect result with every job.

General purpose glues

When convenience and ease of use are more important than strength, satisfactory results can often be achieved by using a general purpose or household adhesive.

These are clear solvent-based adhesives which will stick paper and cardboard, wood, leather, even some plastics, and are used straight from the tube. Check the instructions carefully; some recommend applying the adhesive to both surfaces, others to just one. Whichever method you use, you need to hold or clamp the repair and the adhesive takes some time after assembly to gain full strength. The joint is generally not water or heat-resistant.

Remember that general-purpose adhesives are inflammable and give off unpleasant vapours, so should be used in a well ventilated area. For these reasons they should be kept well out of the reach of children. Most adhesives can be cleaned from your fingers (or anywhere else it gets by mistake) using acetone or nail varnish remover.

Sticking paper and card

Numerous adhesives are specifically for use on paper or card.

Water-based liquid pastes and gums sold in bottles or jars are usually supplied with a spreader or brush. They are simple to apply and safe for children to use, and any excess glue can easily be removed using a slightly damp cloth.

It does have one drawback in that the paper has a tendency to wrinkle as the water dries out.

Stick glue is a semi-solid adhesive that comes in a small cartridge. It is very easy to apply and is suitable for children to use. Remember to replace the top after use or the stick will dry out.

Rubber solution adhesives should be spread on both surfaces; leave until the adhesive is touch-dry and then press the surfaces together. Any surplus dried glue is easily peeled off with your fingers.

Aerosol spray adhesives are easily applied with a sweeping motion. Coat one surface, allow it to dry and then press into place.

Clamping joints

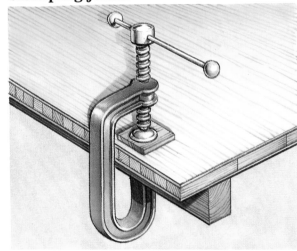

◁ *Glued joints need to be clamped firmly in position while the adhesive dries. This ensures the bond is solid and prevents a gap appearing caused by one side sagging away from the other.*

▽ *Clamps can easily be constructed with a bit of improvisation and some strong string which has little give in it. The string is wrapped around the object once the joints are fitted together, and then drawn tightly to produce a clamping action. The two most effective ways of pulling the string tight are by twisting it with a piece of stick (below left), a technique known as a Spanish windlass, or by using pairs of blocks to give a wedging action (below right). In both cases use tape to hold the tightening devices in position. Always protect the surface with cardboard.*

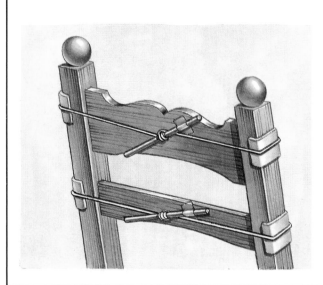

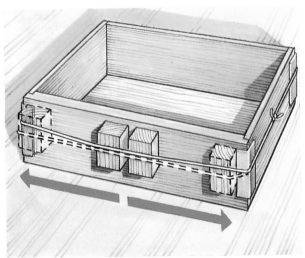

Reinforcing a joint

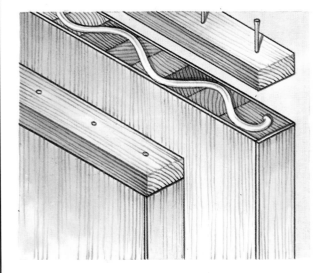

△ *Pins or small-headed nails can be used to reinforce a wooden joint. If they are put in immediately after the glue has been applied, they will also hold it while the adhesive sets.*

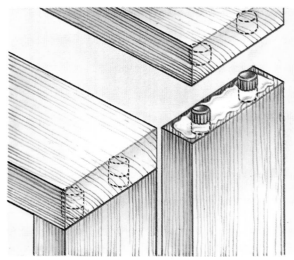

△ *Dowels set into drilled holes are a good way of strengthening glued joints. These are particularly useful when gluing man-made board which would otherwise strain the glue hold.*

Both rubber solution and aerosol adhesives are ideal for covering large areas and give a smoother, more professional finish. However they must be used with care as they give off inflammable vapours, and are unsuitable for children to use.

Reusable adhesives, such as Blutack are similar in appearance to putty. They are easy to peel off and reuse, but they can stain walls and wallpaper if they are left in position for too long.

Adhesives for wood

PVA woodworking adhesive, also known as 'white glue' is the most popular type for general woodwork. It's a milky liquid which will bond softwood, hardwood and all man-made boards, and is colourless when dry.

The joint must be clamped in position for at least two hours until the adhesive hardens. Make sure spills are wiped away with a damp cloth before the adhesive sets.

This type of glue is moderately water-resistant, but prolonged exposure to dampness will result in the bond coming loose.

A heat-resistant and waterproof bond can be achieved by using a brand of adhesive specifically labelled for this task.

There are several types available. Some come as powders which you mix with water, others are packaged as separate powder and hardener to

be mixed in specified quantities.

Once mixed, these adhesives have a limited pot life — in other words, they remain usable for only a short time. This is usually between two and four hours, but check with the manufacturer's instructions.

As with PVA adhesives, for the best results, the joints will need to be clamped until the glue is quite dry.

Adhesives for laminates

Contact adhesives are the most suitable for sticking laminates, and flexible sheet materials such as foam or leather.

The adhesive is spread on both surfaces and is allowed to become touch-dry before the two are pressed together. This needs to be done with extreme care because the resulting bond is instant. Thus the pieces cannot be moved again unless you use a brand which offers a degree of slip (often called a thixotropic adhesive. It is quite heat proof and water-resistant.)

Most contact adhesives are solvent-based, and the fumes are both inflammable and noxious to inhale, so work in a well ventilated area and do not use naked lights. Clean any up spills using the manufacturer's special solvent, or try acetone (nail varnish remover).

Water-based types are also available, and these are much safer and more pleasant to use; spills can be removed with a damp cloth.

Adhesives for plastics

Many plastics are very difficult to stick with adhesives. Two which cannot be stuck satisfactorily by any means are nylon and polythene; they must be fused by heat.

Special vinyl repair adhesive will mend flexible PVC — used for seat covers, sunbeds and beach balls.

Polystyrene cement will mend rigid polystyrene — used for some kitchen and bathroom accessories. However it is not suitable for expanding polystyrene ceiling tiles.

For other plastics, experiment with **epoxy resin adhesives, two-part acrylics** or **cyanoacrylates** (see section below).

Glass, china and metal

There are three types of adhesives available for these materials.

Epoxy resin adhesives are two-part products. Equal quantities of resin and hardener are mixed together, and applied — usually to both surfaces. Quick-setting types set in a few minutes, others take about half an hour for the full bond strength to develop. Once set, the bond is heatproof and waterproof. This type of adhesive can also be used successfully to fill gaps.

However, it does leave a noticeable glue line, which may darken with time. Clean up any spills with white spirit, and trim away any dried adhesive with a well sharpened handyman's knife.

Cyanoacrylate adhesives, also known as superglues, are thin runny liquids which are applied to just one surface. The resulting glue line is very thin, so they are ideal for repairing crockery and glass. One drawback with this adhesive is that it has no gap-filling properties so the parts must be a good fit.

With most brands, the joint is not waterproof, but some are specially formulated for repairing items that will have to be washed or hold liquids, such as mugs and cups.

Avoid skin contact when using this type of adhesive. If you do get your fingers (or anything else) stuck together, immerse them in hot soapy water and peel the stuck areas apart.

Alternatively you can use the manufacturer's release agent if one is supplied with the adhesive.

Two-part acrylics are not mixed directly. You apply adhesive to one surface and hardener to the other, then bring the two together.

This sticks immediately, setting to full strength in a few hours. The adhesive has good heat resistance and is quite waterproof, but doesn't fill gaps very well. Wipe up spills with a dry cloth, trim away any dried adhesive with a sharp knife.

Adhesives for fabrics

The best adhesive for sticking fabrics and carpets is a latex type — a

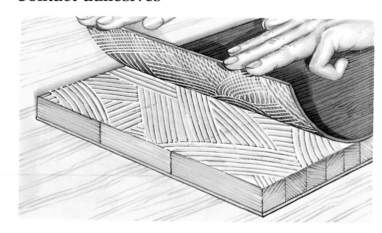

Contact adhesives

△ *Usually used to stick bonding sheet materials to board; make sure the positioning is exact first time.*

With great care, line up the edges of the two materials, and slowly bring together.

white liquid which works like a contact adhesive. Brush adhesive on to the two surfaces, allow them to become touch-dry and then press together. Wipe up any spills that may occur with a damp cloth.

Adhesives for glue guns

Glue guns are electrically-heated tools that take sticks of adhesive. These sticks are melted down and the adhesive is then applied via a nozzle. Initially they were intended

only for woodwork, but a variety of sticks are now available which can be used for general purposes.

Speciality adhesives

Your local DIY store will also sell all sorts of one-job adhesives, clearly labelled as to their purpose. These include wallpaper paste, ceramic tile adhesive, coving adhesive, panel adhesive and so on. You just need to pick out the one appropriate for the job in hand.

This easy-to-use chart will tell you what type of adhesive to use on the various materials in the columns. The materials listed in the left-hand column can be successfully glued to the materials along the top of the chart by using the adhesive (indicated by a number) found where line and column intersect.

	PAPER	WOOD*	MASONRY*	METAL	GLASS	CHINA	PLASTIC*
PAPER	1-7	1,2,7		1,8	1	1	1
WOOD		1,7	10	10			10
STONE		10	10	10			
METAL	1,8	10	10	10-12	10	10	10
GLASS	1		10	10	10-12	10-12	10
CHINA				10	10-12	10-12	10
PLASTIC	1	10		10	10	10	1,8,9 10-12

KEY

1 General-purpose adhesive
2 Liquid paste/gum
3 Stick glue
4 Rubber solution
5 Aerosol adhesive
6 Reusable adhesive
7 Woodworking adhesive
8 Contact adhesive
9 Vinyl repair adhesive
10 Epoxy-resin adhesive
11 Two-part acrylic adhesive
12 Cyanoacrylate adhesive

* WOOD includes man-made boards.
* MASONRY both stone and plaster.
* PLASTIC includes rigid and flexible types and glass fibre.

Maintaining rugs and carpets

*Carpets are one of the most expensive
furnishings required in a home, so it makes sense to look after
them properly. To care for your investment, clean
your carpets regularly and act quickly to remove stains and to
repair small areas of damage.*

Rugs and carpets are hard working textiles which need regular maintenance to keep them in good condition. Stains should be treated immediately as they may be impossible to remove later and damage, such as fraying, should be repaired before it gets worse.

Carpet quality grading

Modern carpets are labelled to show their quality. When examining a carpet, bend the topside of the sample back on itself. In a thick, good quality carpet you will not be able to see the backing. Tug at a couple of tufts to check that they will not come away easily.

Types of carpet fibres

Wool is the traditional carpet fibre. It resists dirt, retains its body and is warm and naturally fire resistant. However, all-wool carpets are expensive. Other natural fibres used are silk and cotton which is not so hard wearing.

Nylon, acrylic and polyester are cheaper than wool but quickly lose their vitality and attract dust and dirt. Carpets with a mixture of wool and man-made fibres offer a happy medium, combining the advantages of each at a reasonable price.

Carpet construction

Carpets are either woven, tufted or bonded. Traditionally the fibres of a carpet were interwoven with the backing to produce a hard-wearing carpet with a long life. Axminster and Wilton carpets are still made in this way. The fibres in a tufted carpet are inserted into a pre-woven backing and held in place by a latex adhesive. A second backing is then added. In bonded carpets the pile is bonded (often heat fused) on to a pre-made backing to produce an inexpensive carpet.

Cleaning carpets

Regular vacuuming helps to remove the grit and dirt that accumulates at the base of a carpet which would otherwise cause wear. Carpets should be shampooed as rarely as possible, because even with modern cleaning methods some shampoo is always left in the carpet and this attracts dirt.

Natural fibre carpets are prone to a certain amount of shrinkage, so they should be treated with care.

When shampooing, use a minimum amount of water and shampoo solution, or use a dry foam type. Hiring a shampoo machine is the best way to clean all your carpets in one go. These machines suck out the shampoo, dirt and grit, leaving the carpet damp rather than wet.

It is important to leave the carpet to dry completely before walking on it; otherwise the pile will be squashed out of shape and dirt will immediately become caught up in the damp fibres.

For a really good clean, have the carpets cleaned by a professional.

Removing burn marks

Flying sparks and cigarette burns can cause unsightly scorch marks. To remove burns, cut out the damaged fibres and replace them with some from a hidden spot. spot.

You will need
◇ Latex adhesive   ◇ Manicure sticks
◇ Tweezers   ◇ Slim craft knife
◇ Piece of card

2 Using the manicure stick, place a dab of adhesive in the bottom of the burn hole. Also apply a tiny blob to the bottom of each tuft of carpet fibres.

1 Use tweezers to tease out the scorched fibres. From another, hidden area of the carpet, remove an equivalent number of matching fibres and place them on the card.

3 When adhesive is touch dry, carefully position each tuft in the hole using tweezers and a clean manicure stick. Push down well. Leave for a few minutes and then trim ends of tufts if necessary.

◆ TIP	SAFETY FIRST

Keep chemicals locked up and out of children's reach. Use with care in a well-ventilated room away from a naked flame and wear rubber gloves.

Patching a fitted carpet

A patch will need to match the design of the damaged area exactly. If you do not have offcuts, consider removing a hidden section of carpet from underneath a piece of furniture.

You will need
◇ Craft knife   ◇ Hessian seaming tape
◇ Long, thin nails   ◇ Brown paper
◇ Latex adhesive   ◇ Hammer

1 Cut a replacement patch of carpet slightly larger than the damaged area. Position it over the damage so that pile and pattern match. Tack down at the corners with nails.

2 Using the patch as a template, cut through the damaged carpet using a craft knife. Make sure the cut is tight in against the sides of the patch to ensure it will fit snugly into the hole created.

3 Take out tacking nails and remove the damaged piece of carpet. Dab latex adhesive around the edge of the patch to stop it fraying.

4 Cut a piece of brown paper slightly larger than the hole and push through. This protects the underlay from adhesive.

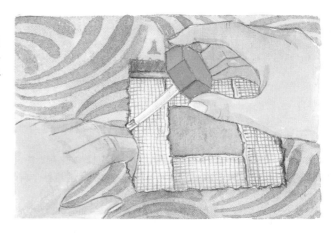

5 Cut four strips of carpet tape slightly longer than the four sides of the hole. Insert through the hole, hessian side up, to frame it. Apply adhesive under edge of carpet and over hessian tape.

6 Apply adhesive to the patch to correspond with the tape. Leave until glue is tacky, then position in hole, matching pattern and pile. Press into position. Tap the edges with a hammer to bond.

7 When dry, tease up fibres around patch edges to hide the join.

Rugs

Most woven and knotted rugs can be vacuumed regularly. Vacuum to within an inch of the edge, but never vacuum over edges or fringes as this causes damage. Brush delicate rugs rather than vacuuming.

If a rug is badly encrusted with dirt, hang it over a strong washing line so that nearly all the rug hangs down on one side. Beat the back with a carpet beater, then vacuum both sides of the rug with the curtain cleaning attachment of the vacuum cleaner.

All rugs should be aired outside from time to time, but should not be left out overnight. They should also be rotated regularly. This prevents one area becoming more worn or faded than another and stops areas of pile becoming permanently marked by furniture.

Spills on valuable rugs

Do not attempt to remove stains from valuable rugs, such as expensive Oriental rugs. If the carpet is not coloured with vegetable dyes, dampen the stain with soda or sparkling water. If the rug has been dyed with vegetable dyes, put a clean, damp white cloth over the stain to absorb it out of the fibres. Take the rug to a professional cleaner as soon as possible.

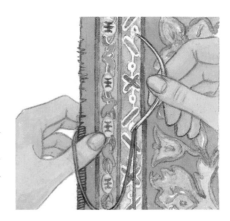

TIP   **SAVE SCRAPS**

If you are having new carpet laid, always keep any small offcuts to repair the carpet in event of an accident. Store these scraps in a handy place and pass them on to the new owner if you move.

Structural damage

As soon as a hole appears in a rug, or an edge starts to fray, get it mended before the damage becomes worse. The edges of rugs are the weak spots which are most likely to become damaged first, so keep an eye on them and make sure that they receive immediate attention when required.

Most repairs to woven and tufted rugs should be left to the professional, but frayed edges on inexpensive rugs can be mended with strong buttonhole thread.

Repairing a frayed edge

Choose yarn in a shade to match the border as closely as possible in colour and thickness. Thread a curved upholsterer's needle with the yarn. Starting about $1\frac{1}{2}$in (4cm) away from damaged area oversew edge and continue the same distance past damage on the far side.

Removing common carpet stains

Most marks will come out if dealt with immediately. Always rinse the area with cool water and dab it as dry as possible after treating (unless product states otherwise). Some strong solvents may take the colour out of the carpet, so you will have to decide whether to put up with a slight stain rather than a faded patch.

Liquid spills Keep a clean absorbent cloth for the job. Rinse out the cloth in warm water and dab the stain. Always use a dabbing motion and a minimum of water to remove as much of the spillage as possible. Do not rub the mark. Wring out the cloth frequently in warm water. Dab dry with kitchen paper.
Solids Scrape up carefully with a palette knife, don't rub in. If a mark remains, treat for the relevant stain.

Stain	Treatment
Blood	Apply cold water to stained area, then blot with cold water in which a few drops of ammonia have been added. Repeat this process as many times as necessary until stain disappears.
Faeces	Remove deposit. Dab with clean warm water. Dab with pet stain remover.
Fruit juice	Blot up excess. Mix 2tsp borax with $\frac{1}{2}$ pint (300ml) warm water. Dab on liberally.
Wine, alcohol	Blot up liquid. Dab with solution of 2tsp borax in $\frac{1}{2}$ pint (300ml) warm water.
Grease, oil	Scrape off excess. Dab with stain removal solvent. Clean with shampoo solution.
Chewing gum	Pick off as much as possible and break up the gum edge with a blunt knife. Place ice cubes in a plastic bag and leave on gum for a couple of minutes to freeze it. When hard, pick remaining gum off with tweezers. Apply stain removal solvent.
Cream, milk	Sponge with warm water, dab dry. Use a stain removal solvent to remove any remaining grease.
Paint	Act immediately and scrape up then blot up excess. Treat water-based paints with water followed by carpet shampoo; treat oil-based paints with white spirit.
Vomit	Scrape up solids then blot liquids. Sponge with I pint carpet shampoo solution, plus I egg cup white vinegar.
Urine	Mop up liquid. Flush with a quick squirt of a soda syphon; dab dry. If stain remains, treat with pet stain remover or 3tbsp salt in I pint (600ml) warm water, followed by I tablespoon ammonia diluted with $\frac{1}{2}$ pint (300ml) water.
Coffee, tea	Blot up all excess liquid with a clean cloth. Dab with warm water. If stain is not removed try the following: on coffee, mix egg yolk with a little warm water, apply to stain; on tea, dab with cloth wrung out in soap and water, then a stain removal solvent. Hot liquid stains are often impossible to remove completely.